M000201560

Sink or Swim?

Sink or Swim?

How God Helps You
Stay Afloat in Adversity

JANE BLAKEWELL

ISBN 978-1-60920-077-0

Printed in the United States of America

©2013 Jane Blakewell

All rights reserved

Library of Congress Cataloging-in-Publication Data

API
Ajoyin Publishing, Inc.
P.O. 342
Three Rivers, MI 49093

www.ajoyin.com

Contents

Foreword

This book is written to give God all the glory for the great things He has done in my life and will continue to do until He calls me home to join Him. In Matthew 5:16, "Let your light shine before men that they may see your good deeds and praise your Father in heaven."

I praise Him for blessing me with wonderful loving parents who became warriors and fighters and who learned how to trust God in their fiery ordeals. They were going to experience many fires as trials lingered, causing their faith to blossom.

I also dedicate this book to my loving husband, Roger, and to my two children, Christopher and Elizabeth. who never gave up believing in my healing. Our church family continually prayed for us which was uplifting and encouraging. Love flowed through family and the church into me, which drew me more to want Jesus as my best friend and Healer.

Introduction

Children learn what they live. Although I didn't have a close, intimate relationship with either of my parents, I knew in my Spirit that there was something very special and unique about both of them. For instance, while in the Navy during World War II, my Dad's ship was bombed and everyone around him perished. Shrapnel struck his entire body, but he remained strong, knowing in his heart he would make it. He received a purple heart. This experience ignited his fighter "sink or swim" spirit.

People are watching and waiting to see how you react in a storm. God is in control and He allows testing to help us grow and mature in Him. Submitting to obedience and accepting trials thrown at you can make life seem to be unfair. However, it can become an open door to help others see the Lord and His mighty acts unfold. His purposes will be made known when life is over.

At times I wondered how long I could stand, while trials continued on for many years. I saw no meaning to anything happening in my life. I wondered if God was upset with me or if I had done something to offend Him. I held onto verses from II Corinthians 12: 9–10. "My grace is sufficient for you, for my power is made perfect in weakness. . . . that is why, for Christ's sake, I delight in weaknesses, in insults, in hardships, in persecutions, in difficulties.

For when I am weak, then I am strong."

Reasons for living became evident when I asked Jesus to be Lord of my life. He would help me live life while choosing to do His will. There will always be difficulties for Christians who dedicate their lives to servant hood. Giving up and sinking is never the way out. It is better to give to others than to receive anything for yourself.

I have spoken to groups and written short articles about my personal testimonies and victories God has blessed me with. These stories have uplifted many people who have suggested I write a book, which the devil let me know for years I could never do. I now take that challenge seriously. I want to bless the Lord of glory and give others encouragement so they can watch their dreams come true.

Part One

THE ACCIDENT

═══════════

Chapter 1

The Neighbor's Pool

I grew up in Flossmoor, Ill., about 25 miles south of Chicago. I was blessed with loving parents and a big brother, Tom. I always enjoyed singing and when I was 14, I had an opportunity to be in the eighth grade operetta, "The Pirates of Penzance," in which I was Ruth. Music is a gift from God and He would be using it in my life in a very special way.

Swimming and water sports were always a high priority and any time there was a pool or lake around, I was in it. Sinking was never a word in my vocabulary. You couldn't keep me out of it, for water was part of my being. My Mom's friend taught me to swim when I was eight, and my uncle taught me to water ski soon after. Years later I would water ski to work while lifeguarding on a beach in Lake Geneva, Wis.

People were always challenging me to try new things. I was asked by close friends of my parents to care for their pool and horses for a long weekend.

As a 14-year old, I thought I was ready to handle any challenge. Taking on this job was exciting. What would come out of this ordeal while doing the job would change my destiny. My precious care-free life was about to be turned upside down.

I had ridden their horses occasionally, but the best part of the job was their pool. On a hot day in July 1962 I invited a few friends over to swim. We all were having fun doing stunts and crazy dives. Trying to come out as a winner, I decided to do a sailor dive with my arms at my side and went in head-first. It was totally wrong but I had watched others try with success. No one was being very careful, and where I went in, it was only four feet deep.

I truly do not remember what happened after the dive. I must have come up and been able to get out of the pool by myself. My friends must not have been concerned about me, because no one called for help, which would have changed the outcome drastically. They all went home, so I was alone. My teeth/nasal area of my face, hit the bottom hard, and was now open to infection.

About two days after the accident, my parents returned home and came to get me at the pool house. They had no idea what they would experience when they walked into the house. I was told that I was sprawled out on the floor screaming and yelling while having a grand mal seizure. I was hallucinating and totally unaware of my circumstances.

They called an ambulance immediately and were

horrified at what they were seeing. Their beautiful, healthy, young daughter was now at the mercy of God alone. Their peace was now shattered. Panic and fear were written all over their faces while in a state of shock. What had really caused this disaster? Our three doctors worked at the Michael Reese Hospital in Chicago, where I would remain for a lengthy stay.

I was told by a close friend who had sent this message to my parents, assuring them that "God was in control. Nothing alarms Him or takes Him by surprise. Nothing is too big for Him to handle or so small it escapes His attention. When the winds of the world begin to blow, He remains seated. When raging waves surround us, He governs their temper. We need not be moved, because the Lord is seated and sovereign."

For many years I asked questions about my hospital stay and illness. I heard many partial stories from friends and relatives. No one really wanted to talk about it. Mom lived through every minute of the crisis and just thinking about it upset her. And Dad couldn't talk about it either. So this part of my life was hidden for a long time. Very slowly, pieces of the puzzle started to fit together to make the picture more clear.

Praise God, I never was aware of my illness or any of the horrors my parents experienced. My Mom's friend shared a few memories of how my Mom was strong through it all, and how my Dad held her up.

Years later I requested medical record papers from that Chicago hospital, hoping it could clear up some questions I would always have. Unfortunately, when they came, the writing had faded and was very hard to read. Bits and pieces were legible, like the shallow dive had broken my nose, and my teeth were all knocked loose. The orthodontist had taken my braces off as I lay unconscious in the hospital.

I have been told that mosquitoes that were present near the pool carry the encephalitis virus and it was likely that I could have been bitten by one of those infected bugs. My fever sky-rocketed to over 107 degrees and would not break. Lengthy severe grand mal seizures continued day and night. My brother told me I lay on a bed of ice and was firmly strapped in, since seizures continued and I shook all the time. The ice surrounded me.

The doctors gave my parents no hope and told them many times I would not live. They asked them to prepare for my death. God seemed to have a different idea and kept me alive, despite what doctors told them. God determines life's decisions and His will was being carried out. God saw good things happening. God answers prayers.

The part of my brain that was affected was the meninges, which is the memory area. The doctors did not believe healing was possible. They said if I lived, I would be institutionalized, having uncontrolled seizures and severe mental disabilities. My doctors were going to experience God in a new way.

How or why God chose to break my high fever would remain a mystery.

My parents were weary, but settling for a partial victory was not part of the game. God never stops at half a victory. When you are ready to sink, it is often the moment that the breakthrough could come. They may have been emotionally exhausted, but they never lost hope. They had to avoid doubt and false thinking.

Chapter 2

Music for Healing

Since my memory of the time following the accident is sketchy, my brother was able to fill in some of the blanks years later. "I vividly recall your singing in the hospital room at the top of your lungs," he said, "which included many Gilbert and Sullivan songs and other show tunes. I recall that when Mom, Dad and I were visiting you with Dr. Bell, our minister, he would intentionally tell jokes in the hall outside your room to try to lift our spirits. I was most afraid when you were in the hospital. We really thought you could possibly die."

After hearing that I actually sang while I was unconscious really excited me. I began to see how my love for singing caused a major healing in my life. I had always assumed that playing records after my homecoming was the way my memory was restored. God had carefully protected and caressed the small area of my brain, holding it lovingly in His hands, so that no more damage could occur. He used my love for music to keep my memory alive and well. How awesome!

I have been told I had been released from the hospital too early. Mom and Dad had their hands full. My high fever was gone but another miracle happened. The seizures stopped. As time went by, doctors realized this was true. They cautiously halted the medication just to see if I was really free of seizures. Doctors warned my parents seizures could start again, just from stress. They were told to watch me very carefully.

I had lost weight lying motionless for more than three months and really could not walk well until the muscles became strong again. I have no recollection of having therapy at all. When I came home, I laid on the couch all day. I had no guests because I had no idea who they were. I didn't know who my own parents were at first. I needed to be watched, as my body grew in strength. I was told I ran out in the streets like a wild animal let out of a cage.

The high fever caused scarring, leaving my brain functioning as a two-year old. I was afraid of people. I was strong-willed and nothing was going to stop me from going forward. I had no awareness about my illness and near-death experience. It was dangerous for everyone caring for me causing all to wonder if I should really live at home.

Thanks to family, friends and prayers, it was obvious that God was not going to let me sink. Music continually playing throughout the house lifted everyone's spirits. These were musicals I memorized. Within a few months words came back quickly. Within a few months doctors tested to see if school was a possibility again.

My brother said, "Everyone involved, including the doctors, were totally amazed at how quickly things came back. They said different parts of my brain were functioning in ways they had never thought possible."

Chapter 3

My New Class

The in-depth testing the doctors did for me showed education was again possible and the brain was mending faster than imagined. I went to the high school and attended a few classes to see how I would respond. All the students' faces were new to me. It was hard to explain that I had been ill and missed over a year of school.

The school board set up a "school-to-home" telephone system. I could sit at our dining room table and press buttons when I knew the right answer to questions and then take part in the discussions. I could hear the class while in session, which was amazing for 1963. I felt encouraged and excited, as were the doctors and teachers. I was determined to find out who I was and what had happened to that missing part of my life. I was keenly aware something did not seem right.

My parents were given the name of a child psychologist in downtown Chicago. The doctors wanted me to visit and talk out what had taken place during the last year. Mom had to let me go out into the real world by letting me take a train to downtown Chicago by myself. Doctors were confident that I could handle it. It was good medicine for both of us.

The doctors' plan worked, for I was happier, relaxed and enjoying life. Going to new classes and meeting new friends who cared proved very helpful. My social life came back quickly. I had a few friends who walked me through the rest of high school. There was only one way to go and that was forward. Giving up and sinking was not part of the big game.

I had smashed my face on the pool bottom which caused breathing problems for me. It called for painful nasal surgery. They put bandages on before I saw what I looked like, so one day I took them off myself. That was not a good idea! They tried to reset it, but I would need more surgery in later life. Impatience brought me many problems.

My favorite class in high school was Viking Choir. Music was my first love and words came easily. I could pick up a tune and have words already in my head . . . a real gift. We sang psalms, hymns and spiritual songs. God had used music for my healing. A beautiful new life was emerging in me as I learned how to praise the Lord.

I also loved synchronized swimming class. I was like a fish in water and we had fun learning new stunts but safely this time. Water was a best friend.

As I got better, my father was diagnosed with

throat cancer and had his larynx removed. They had no recorders for speaking as they do now, so he learned the technique of esophageal speaking, the art of swallowing air and burping out sounds to speak words. He had to slowly enunciate each letter sound.

Dad's fighter spirit remained faithful to the end. I was unaware of the horror and fear that filled my parents' lives during his recovery. I was just trying to keep going forward in my own little world. I heard when you experience severe stress it can wear down your physical being. Some believed my illness brought his cancer on. I hoped this was not true. Other environmental factors, including his drinking and smoking, could have been factors. I knew not to blame myself.

He courageously visited me daily while I was deathly ill. He never gave up and believed I would be fine. I never questioned him about how he handled all this. How Mom also had the ability to stand firm was amazing to me. First my illness and then Dad's.

My parents needed a close relationship with Jesus and learn to rejoice when things looked black, which seemed ridiculous. Where was God? He was behind the curtains, directing and overseeing it all. My parents were trusting and believing they'd see God show His divine character and see an eventual victory. Genesis 18:14 states, "Is anything too hard for the Lord?"

Romans 5:3–4 also states, "We rejoice in our sufferings because we know that suffering produces perseverance; perseverance, character; and character, hope."

Mom and Dad kept marching forward. They had a strong character and willingness to wait, though there seemed to be no end in sight. Looking from the outside in, they were confidently peaceful, but inwardly, a major battle raged on. They had to walk by faith. Hebrews 11:1 states, "Faith is being sure of what we hope for and certain of what we do not see."

My hospital stay put a financial strain on my parents, so Dad needed a better job where speaking was not important. My uncle in Wisconsin offered him a job managing his four retail stores as he had done in Chicago. The stores thrived while Dad had the position.

I was about to be a senior in high school when my parents had to move to Wisconsin for his new job. I would now need to start over in a new high school, leaving my new-found friends I had grown to love behind. My parents did not want me to suffer hardships because of their move.

A close single friend of my Mom's, Evelyn, offered me a place to stay in her home during my senior year. My parents could now go to Lake Geneva, Wis., in peace, knowing I was cared for without their need to worry. My maturity level thrived and I was ready to be on my own. They made decisions for me many years and now I would be set free to learn what God had in store for me.

Tests, homework and studying became easy for me. I got involved in activities after school and enjoyed freedom driving and making my own decisions. Seniors in my high school asked where are you going to school, not are you going. Since my parents were now Wisconsin residents, I chose the University of Wisconsin–Eau Claire. While visiting the Eau Claire campus for the first time, I loved the location on the Chippewa River, winding through the campus and downtown. I could get exercise daily by just going to classes and to stores downtown with no need for a car.

God was granting me a future with no need to tread water. I was ready to walk on water. I had developed a new boldness and confidence in myself. My new life was exciting and all who prayed for me got to see the victory. Philippians 3:13 states, "But one thing I do; forgetting what is behind and straining toward what is ahead, I press on toward the goal to win the prize for which God has called me."

Chapter 4

Off to College

This was now the fall of 1967. No one at the university knew anything about my past. Everyone at home knew too much. I never realized how college may have not been an option for me. God had me prepared for college without much difficulty. Classes went well and teachers were fantastic. I had missed only a year of high school and I never had need for any kind of tutoring.

My roommate from Milwaukee majored in elementary education. She put up with childish pranks I pulled for fun like everyone in the dorms. I looked forward to meeting new people and had a few dates. Nothing developed into anything serious. Campus life was exciting and very busy, but I also looked forward to summers and being home. Summer was a time all college kids needed to freshen up and relax.

My cousin Linda and I worked in her father's retail store. We had fun selling and buying clothes for ourselves. Linda's boyfriend, John, wanted to visit her from Wausau, a town in north central Wisconsin. God had all the playing pieces marked out at this time. His plan had my name written all over it. Psalm 139: 16 states, "That all the days ordained for me were written in your book before one of them came to be."

John's car did not travel long distances, so he asked his friend, Roger Blakewell, if he would drive his car to the resort town of Lake Geneva. Roger worked at Wausau Insurance and was a few years older than me. He told John he would be glad to do it, but could he ask his girlfriend to find him a date. So they came into the store and Roger's eyes met mine and it was love at first sight. We had a wonderful time, laughing, dancing and sharing stories together. Linda never saw John again, but Roger and I kept writing for the rest of the summer.

When I went back to school in the fall, it was now easier getting together. Eau Claire was just a few hours away from Wausau so we could be together more often. We wrote daily and spent time together on many weekends. He stayed in the men's dorms and I found rides to Wausau and stayed at his parents' house where he lived.

Roger had completed just two years of college and went back to work again. I suggested that he return to school and get his degree. I had just two years left and then we could graduate together in 1971. He decided to do it and commuted daily to the University of Wisconsin–Stevens Point with a few other students. He worked on an English major with a history minor. We continued writing and calling long distance. We were together most weekends and studied together.

When I became a senior, I started student teaching. I worked with sixth graders at a school located off campus. I walked daily from the dorms and enjoyed getting to know the kids. I later worked and taught at the campus elementary school with third graders. I liked the younger children. Teaching was easy for me because I had taught swim classes.

The university had just completed an Olympic pool on upper campus for lap swimming, where I spent a lot of time. I enjoyed upper campus living where all the action was. We climbed over 150 steps to get up to the dorms. Administration canceled many winter classes because the wind chill factor was too bitter. It made it difficult to breathe normally because temperatures dropped far below zero, and snow fell an average of 100 inches. Winter carnival included snow sculptures designed by students. Many were painted cartoon characters or animals, some being 15 feet tall.

School was a joy for me and I was now a new person; the old Jane had disappeared. College was a high point in my life. I enjoyed learning and I loved summers that were exciting with my new job with the water safety patrol, as a lifeguard on a small beach on Lake Geneva. I had met two special young girls who sat with me daily. My Dad took me to work on my water ski, dropping me off near my pier.

Life was great. I was a senior in college and thinking about my future. Roger and I planned on being married after graduation in June 1971. He asked my Dad for permission to marry me and Dad smiled and nodded yes. It was something they never imagined could happen. We asked the young girls from my pier to be in the wedding and we started planning where it would be hosted.

Chapter 5

My New Life Begins

Though my parents were living in Lake Geneva, I wanted to be married in Flossmoor, with friends who had prayed for my life to be restored. Mom's friends organized a small reception in the church basement. There were tears of great joy seeing how God brought us together. We decided to move away from Wausau and found jobs in the Chicago area. I was a year-round substitute teacher and Roger worked for his former employer, prior to finishing college.

We had a company car, so Roger dropped me off at the schools and picked me up when the day was done. He drove to businesses in the Chicago suburbs. Later he was transferred to Fort Wayne, Ind., doing the same work. Full-time teaching positions did not exist. I subbed again, never having a chance to be creative. Roger always wanted to use his English degree, writing in a communications department. Traveling daily in the car was stressful and not enjoyable.

Our friends were buying homes, so we chose to follow suit. We found a lovely Lutheran church in our neighborhood. It was a blessing for me, for I had no background in church as Roger had with family members in the ministry. I had been part of Campus Crusade for Christ in college, where I learned about Jesus and making Him the main part of my life.

We lived in our new home only nine months when an unexpected call came from Wausau Insurance, letting Roger know there was a writing job open. After the interview in Wisconsin, near where his parents lived, he accepted the job. I was happy for him, but deep down inside I was stressed out knowing my comfort zone would disappear. We would leave our friends, house and subbing jobs. Inwardly, I was worried about his Dad and our uneasy relationship. This big move would cause problems that neither of us could ever have imagined.

After living in Wisconsin for a few months, a close friend from Fort Wayne shared that she had noticed me blankly staring at times. It bothered her enough to call me and ask if Roger had actually seen it himself. It happened quite infrequently and really unnoticeable to most anyone. Roger was at work and enjoying time with me after a long day at work. Hearing her message was important but having never seen it himself, he dismissed it. I was totally unaware of it.

It had now been over 12 years since my lengthy stay in the hospital with encephalitis in Chicago. We had cancelled possibilities about seizures recurring. I went through college, married three years, and walked into new classrooms without lesson plans. It seemed nothing could trigger seizure activity again. However, the neurologists cautioned my parents that it was possible. These blank stares seemed harmless, but we would learn there are different kinds of seizures, unlike the ones I had while unconscious.

Part Two

BIG CHANGES

Chapter 6

Trouble in Wausau

It was now the winter of 1974. Wausau had no subbing or teaching jobs. The houses were more expensive and had less to offer. Our move in April arrived and leaving friends expecting babies made the move even worse. I was headed to the frozen north woods without a job or close friends. This new house was a tri-level with ugly carpet and no fireplace. This move was celebrating his new job and our new life ahead. I wanted no changes and life to be as it had been in Indiana.

It was April now and there were teacher aide jobs only, so I found a lifeguard supervisor job starting June 8. We moved in a huge April snow storm with our two cats. All our furniture fit well and I had no real reason to complain. Roger was at work with our car, so the days grew long. There were no young neighbors to reach out to either. Roger knew the town well and tried to tell me how easy it was going anywhere from our house.

I could not wait to start this new job in June. While Roger was at work, no one was aware what was happening at home. I found large bruises all over my body, having no idea why. It didn't seem to bother me, nor did I share my concern with Roger. The house did have many stairs, but I did not remember falling or bumping into anything.

The first day of my lifeguard job finally arrived. It had been a long winter and freedom to work a job I could enjoy seemed exciting. I left the house under stress, wondering how to get there and be on time. As I approached an intersection, a seizure occurred and my body fell into the steering wheel. My foot hit the accelerator as I fell forward, causing the car to speed up and go right into the river.

This new type seizure was called complex partial. The seizure comes from both sides of the brain and there is no awareness of it coming on or having happened. Some victims are aware and can feel a seizure coming on, sit down prior to it, and are safe from a fall. God was not going to let me drown or allow my car to sink too deeply until help arrived. The car was now immersed half-way, at an angle. I had no idea that there had been an accident.

Coming out of the unconscious state while still under water, I'll never forget seeing the wide staring eyes glaring at me. His hand was moving in circles, motioning me to roll down the window. I was really panic-stricken coming out of the seizure, and did what I could. Because electric windows were not involved, I was able to get the tiny back window open wide enough for this man to pull me out.

Witnesses told the police that my rescuer just happened to be following me that Saturday morning at 8 o'clock. When I drove in, he pulled off the road and jumped into the river. Coming out of my groggy state, I was now focusing on things prior to the accident, knowing I would be late to my meeting. I was not focused on what had happened and what could have happened if this man had not been there. I was soaking wet, but I insisted the police take me to the meeting. I was greeted and insensitively known as "the lifeguard who teaches cars to swim." They had heard about the accident on the radio and thought it was funny.

Psalm 18:6 was a message of faith for me at this pivotal time in my life. "In my distress I called to the Lord; I cried to God for help. From His temple he heard my voice; my cry came before him" and verse 16 continues, "He reached down from on high and took hold of me; he drew me out of deep waters." Although I was totally unaware of danger happening, it all comes to a head. God watches over His children, I did not have a close intimate relationship with Him, but He was there because He loved me.

Bad news travels fast. This accident ended my job, and my self-worth plummeted. Roger had been mowing the grass when I had left and the police now brought me home soaking wet. The next morning two policemen came to our front door, and asked for my driver's license. It was ripped in half in front of me and I was told to stay off the roads.

Now it all made sense. I did have seizures. The bruises had come from my having fallen down the stairs while experiencing a seizure. I just got up and kept going after a fall, having no idea why I was on the ground.

We met new doctors the next day. My charts from Chicago arrived and our small town doctors had no idea what to do. There were very few drugs for seizure disorders and most had bad side-effects. The one drug that could have worked caused my body to be covered with a rash. The drug does damage to the liver, so I am thankful I was allergic to it.

I never wanted to move to Wisconsin and now I really hated everything about it. God had protected me from harm and a near drowning. I believe in angels and feel the man at the river side had been placed there just for me. Before we had an opportunity to thank him, he died suddenly. Indeed, he may have been my angel! And perhaps my experience could help me share miracles in my life with others who are fighting major battles and give them hope.

Chapter 7

Baby Makes Three

Years of trying new drugs with bad side effects continued. I needed shots into welts to rid swelling damages that certain drugs caused. It was painful and horrible. I was overdosed most of the time, was dizzy, spaced out and my vision was impaired. Each time a seizure happened, doctors increased the dose, hoping it would stop them. More seizures can happen because of overdosing.

Roger left me alone daily so he could work and support us. I was drugged enough to keep me safe. I kept cooking, cleaning, sewing clothes and making craft items. I was thrilled when Roger came home, though all we did was go to the doctor's office or grocery store. I depended on everyone so I could function.

People at the Lutheran church were afraid of seizures and stayed far away from me. I needed friends and love. Our neighborhood had elderly rich folks, but no younger friends like there had been in

Chicago and Fort Wayne. No children ran outside in the area and our neighborhood seemed lifeless.

Roger and I realized I needed something to keep me happier and content, since teaching was no longer possible. We decided having a baby would take care of my loneliness. My seizure drugs could cause conflict with my hormones and possibly damage the fetus, but that was something we never believed would happen. Doctors told us we should wait until the seizures were more controlled. Safety was their reason, but I had no patience, plenty of time, and I wanted a baby.

Within the year, we were blessed with a healthy baby boy and named him Christopher, born in December 1975. All seemed to be going very well. He was perfect in every way and we enjoyed being new parents. Roger traveled rarely with his new job, but when he was gone, my peace disappeared. I had fear knowing I'd have no ride to get to a doctor if an accident happened. His parents said they would never babysit, unless there were severe circumstances. I believe his Mom would have loved it, but his Dad decided everything.

I had occasional seizures, but never once did I fall with Chris in my arms. Being a first-time Mom, I was not aware of "postpartum" depression that can come on after six weeks. My hormones were working overtime and seizure drugs only made things worse.

I remember fearing the worst one time when Chris rolled over quickly and fell off the bed. I thought I he was hurt badly and I blamed myself. Frightened, I called Roger's parents, so his Dad came over to get both of us. He realized something was wrong, for I could not calm down. He called an ambulance and I was admitted into the psych ward. My hormones went crazy and I was now experiencing a psychotic breakdown.

His parents did babysit for about six weeks, at least until I was well enough to be a mom again. I had long hours of therapy, new medications and talk sessions. I grew strong again mentally and we realized what the doctors had said made sense.

Some friends we had known in Chicago suggested that we go to the City of Faith in Tulsa, Okla., for faith-based treatment and prayer. They paid for the trip and his parents cared for Chris. I was admitted to the hospital and Roger stayed at a nearby hotel for about a week.

The Tulsa staff prayed with wisdom as to what God had in mind for healing. The experience just by itself was healing and my spirit was lifted up. The drugs were finally in my system and my body was reacting well to the new change.

My local doctors told us I would never be the same after the severe breakdown, but they were wrong again. The treatment and care in Tulsa helped a great deal. They told me God was the Great Physician and His plans were only for my good. God always has different plans than medical doctors. God will always be the Great Physician.

Chapter 8

A Girl Named Lori

I hosted many Bible studies at our house and learned from many women who loved the Lord. I enjoyed entertaining guests and serving treats to them. God was there in the middle of all our discussions. I was growing spiritually and reading the Bible on my own. Our family went to church, but members had their own cliques and lived in their own worlds. We had no warm relationships with anyone. But God had plans to help me find out who I was and how I could be used to help Him.

There was a major piece of my life about to unfold that would unlock all sorts of problems that kept me bound. After a sermon ended, the pastors added a prayer with a few words that cut through me like a knife. The prayer was for Lori who had been in an auto accident. She was still unconscious after three months with encephalitis. This totally amazed me that anyone could have my illness. I wanted to see her and let her parents know they should not give up hope.

This prayer continued weekly until I told Roger I had to go to the hospital. I went to the desk and asked for her room in ICU, where no one was able to go except for close relatives and friends. I boldly walked right through the double doors and found her in her cubicle as she lay unconscious.

It was a flashback of what my parents had on their plate when coming to see me. A nurse chased me out of the ICU. I had seen just enough to satisfy my questioning mind. I went into the waiting room and asked if Lori's parents were there, because I had not met them before.

A tall, distressed lady stood up with fear written all over her face. Crying had made her face swollen and her eyes were bloodshot. She told me she was Mary Prigge and wondered why I was there. I told her we had heard weeks of prayer for her daughter at our church and I had come only to share "good news" that I'd had Lori's illness. Doctors gave my parents no hope but they had been wrong in their diagnosis.

Mary grabbed and hugged me tightly and would not let go. I had no idea what to expect and I was forever grateful I was able to lighten their heavy load. She told me Lori had been in a head-on collision with a huge truck on a rainy night. The driver could not stop and Lori's head went right through the windshield and had immediate brain surgery. The deadly virus entered her incision. The muscle control area in her brain was severely damaged.

After becoming conscious after a few months, she was paralyzed from the neck down.

Her damaged tongue muscle made it almost impossible to talk. She was very angry about her newfound life and wondering how to deal with it. Her beautiful face and body were mangled and she was told that healing would never come. She didn't want visitors. Her family had no idea how to uplift her distressed spirit.

When she heard her Mom tell her about my dive and having had encephalitis, and doing well, she showed interest in meeting me. I was surprised after hearing such negative thoughts about her "throwing in the towel" that she even cared about getting better. I was thrilled to have this opportunity to help, but inwardly wondering if I would have the right words and know what to say when she could not answer back. Initially fearful of uncertainty, I desired to reach out in love and see her walk out as a healed young woman. I had a positive attitude and was trusted that God could make this work.

When Lori was released from the hospital, her Mom asked if they could come to our house for a visit. Doctors talked about therapy classes so I suggested swimming would be great for her. Lori quickly wrote on her word board, "I am afraid of water!" I told her I could teach her to swim. I learned that the county health care therapy pool was available every morning. It was Olympic size and the water temperature about 90 degrees. I was unable to drive, so a medical van picked me up with Lori.

I hadn't heard about the therapy pool, so this was an open door in my eyes for her healing. There were handicapped young people in the locker room, with limbs missing and heredity diseases with no cures. They were laughing and enjoying time together. Real people. I wheeled her chair down into the pool and Lori kept grabbing me tightly. She later realized if she relaxed, she could float. We learned together and laughed a lot, while her muscles were slowly getting stronger because of direct water pressure on them.

We went daily for many months as her muscles grew stronger. People in church showed more interest in me, now that I had a major role to play. My self-worth was coming alive, for helping hurting people was my new-found gift. I was helping Lori with my swimming expertise. She graduated from the wheel chair to a walker, and then a few months later, she felt she could handle a cane.

Having been afraid of water, Lori now trusted me enough to let go and try it out. She knew I really cared and I wanted a victory for both of us to see her walk like she had prior to the accident. The final stage was learning to steady herself with weight on both legs to hold her up. The victory day at church finally came as she stood up by herself and then walked up a few stairs to the church altar and knelt for communion. The congregation stood up and applauded!

God let the church see a new part of me never

exposed. I had always been the "woman with seizures" who never talked. I now had a changed personality, a boldness to help and give it all I had to make it work. People knew and recognized that they could never have done it themselves. What a gift God gave me, using swimming talents to give a wheelchair-bound, frightened young girl strength in her body and hope for the future. Lori's story was published in the *Pentecostal Evangel* in 1994.

When I got stronger and surer of myself, Roger drove me to an epilepsy support group, which strengthened me and helped many others. I found many who suffered with the same emotional traumas I had and we all listened to each other and tried to give loving advice. Most of the time, all you needed to do was listen. Getting rides to and from meetings were a big thing to all of us. God always found ways for us to be together.

At this same time I heard that the author Joni Eareckson, who also experienced a serious diving accident, was coming to the nearby Marshfield Arena to speak. She had always been a hero to me. Roger wanted to take me and Lori to hear her testimony. However, I was unable to reach Lori on the phone to tell her about it. As we drove into the parking lot, we were pleased to see Lori and her parents' van pulling up next to us. We all heard Joni speak and it was a wonderful message to lift our spirits. Afterwards, we finally met Joni. I still have a photo of her writing a message of hope, with a pen in her mouth, to Lori.

It was thrilling for both of us.

Chapter 9

Being a Mom

Roger and I enjoyed time together and had fun with the new baby, Christopher. Just feeding him, watching him crawl and slowly get back up again, and learning to walk, was totally amazing. Meals were always fun and when we took him out to eat, he always had people come up and say hi and tell him how cute he was. He was very social and still is today. He had curly blond hair. We finally had to get him a haircut, for everyone always was asking "what's her name" even while wearing blue.

Although having a baby did cause medical problems, it was a good thing, no matter who told us differently. Doctors were totally against it and everyone we asked thought it would be too hard for me to handle. Sure, I did have a post-partum breakdown and I was very sick for a few months. Roger's parents cared for him, like they said they would in emergencies. I was stronger and healthier now and baby Chris kept me quite busy.

Days flew by, though I do not recall much that went on. It was a blessing for me to have a child to care for. Chris was a beautiful gift from God. I did enjoy motherhood and have many happy memories of it. It also gave Roger joy coming home to a little one, instead of just dwelling on my illness and worrying about me and drug reactions. Chris blessed us with happiness and challenges. When decisions had to be made, we consulted doctors or other parents as to how to handle certain unusual circumstances.

Doctors and friends all suggested moving closer to town so I could have more freedom with the city bus service available to me. Although it was a good idea, we didn't do it, because it was unsafe for both Chris and me. I could have had a seizure on the bus or got lost, and then we would have missed the bus or an appointment we were trying to get to on time.

However, we kept very active despite my seizure problem. We started cross-country skiing together when Chris was three. We loved camping in tents and cooking out in the north woods. As I look back, I am thrilled we did all we did. I never was worried about falling because I was never aware a seizure was about to happen. I never thought about what people could see or say, for I just blacked out. I never dwelt on negatives or I would have wanted to stay home and hide in shame.

God did not want kind of life for me, so I was totally able to enjoy all of life, even though there were going to be many more deep valleys. However, after any valley experience, the only way is up and mountaintops are great to look forward to. We eventually did move to another neighborhood where God had planned for us to be. He always had our best interest at heart throughout our lives.

Winter was always long and being trapped in the house with a three-year-old was hair-raising. Bitter cold with ice and snow made it difficult for any young Mom with a small child. The house we had was now lovely, for we had built a fireplace, had done much for the baths, kitchen and bedrooms along with gardens and exterior of the house. We loved being on the lake and near a golf course. The bus service was over a mile away, and just walking to school or downtown took forever. There were no young couples or children around either. After deciding to sell it, we found a realtor who told us we would have no problems just because of the house location.

We put it on the market and it sold within the first month. We were totally surprised but we now had to move to a small apartment complex 15 miles south of us. We put some furniture in storage until we found a house where all we owned would fit. My Mom gave us her baby grand piano, so that added to the problem for finding the perfect house. After months of looking and almost desperate to get out of the tiny apartment, we finally found one. However, this house was now farther from schools and the city, but it was a younger neighborhood than the first house, which had been the main purpose for our decision to move at all.

God does work in mysterious ways. We had no clue what was about to unfold. This new house was ranch style and located in a beautiful area with woods, wild flowers and wildlife everywhere, and at the right price. We were tired of looking at houses and living so far away from everything, so we bit the bullet and bought it. Everything about the house seemed wrong from the beginning. The dark carpet color, dark wood paneling everywhere, bad windows, and no air conditioning were not our first choices while looking for the right place.

We learned to live with the problems and worked things out to make it better, watching carefully the costs of doing anything before we did it. I really enjoyed challenges and it worked well to make my days fly by faster. When Chris took naps, I got very creative with my abilities for wallpapering over ugly dark paneling, which brightened the house. I sewed short curtains for the bedrooms and drapes for the living and dining rooms. I started slipcovering older furniture which amazed me that I would even tackle such a task. Roger came home to see my new creations and was pleased with all of it.

We decided Chris needed a baby sister, despite what the doctors said. Elizabeth was born healthy and beautiful. Chris, now four, was jealous of her from day one. I had no idea how to handle his reactions to having the new baby taking much of his attention away. I needed his help to care for her, but he wanted no part of it. He wanted diapers again and refused naps. I had seizures throughout my whole pregnancy, because I stopped drugs so I could try nursing her. It was enjoyable for a time, but seizures continued and it wasn't safe anymore. We enjoyed life with two children, and life was full and very busy.

I was having emotional difficulties, because of drugs and hormonal changes in my body. When Elizabeth was about six weeks old, I had a minor setback, but things cleared up quickly. Our home church had still not befriended me and there was no promise of my ever finding a close friend to confide in. My life had a very empty void no one could fill. I was depressed and lonely. God knew I was in great need and He was about to make my life turn upside-down.

I needed a partial hysterectomy after her birth which turned into a real blessing for me. The surgeons had found cancer cells forming in the uterus, so we were glad it was removed. We never thought of having more than two children anyway. The whole idea that we had been blessed with two healthy children at all when we were told not to have children was truly amazing and illustrated God's great love and compassion.

Chapter 10

My New Church

I was invited to many Bible studies people had at their homes, but transportation was always a problem. So I invited people to come to our house for sharing Jesus and to enjoy friends. Cindy, our babysitter for the kids during the studies, had seen my hurting spirit and invited me to come to her Sunday night church service. I was thrilled just getting out of the house. Roger and I had no idea how this service would change my life quickly.

This church was not Lutheran but an Assembly of God church. When Cindy and I walked in, I was greeted with smiles and open arms. I was the center of attention and treated like a queen. From having no self-worth and being used to rejection from anyone at our home church, I was now truly elated. I felt important and loved. They wanted to know all about me and hear about my family and earlier life. They were thrilled I came. I felt their love flow out of them into me

Because it was a Pentecostal church, the people responded to the music by clapping hands and raising their arms in praise. What seemed special was they sang scripture over and over, making it easy to memorize. There was a reading from the Bible and sometimes it was scripture from the song we had just sung. The service had no actual format. It was completely Spirit-led and could possibly be only praise and worship, without a sermon.

I stood and watched everyone, totally amazed, but really having no idea why they were doing what they did. I enjoyed their enthusiasm, liveliness and excitement during the service. It was completely different than anything I had ever experienced at church. I enjoyed the beautiful hymns at our home church, .because they were lovely and meaningful, but this new music was vibrant and unique. They also sang lovely, quiet, deeply spiritual songs that spoke directly to your heart that could cause tears.

Lyrics were shown on the large overhead screen. The tunes were catchy, because even after coming home, the songs would come back and I found myself singing them. The sermons were straight to the point and easy for me to understand. The services ended with an altar call and prayers for healing. The pastor prayed, "If you have not asked Jesus to be Lord of your life, now was the time, and to please come up for prayer." I asked Cindy if I could go and she nodded yes. I ran up there quickly. I had given my life to Jesus in college at Campus Crusade for

Christ. I had never understood the true meaning of what I had done. Now I was aware of the real meaning and I was ready to walk through the salvation message again, knowing I really wanted and needed Him in my life.

After the salvation call, the pastor or elders in the church had prayers for those who wanted healing. They used anointing oil on your forehead or hands. James 5:14–15 clearly states, "Are any of you sick? He should call the elders of the church to pray over him and anoint him with oil in the name of the Lord. And the prayer offered in faith will make the sick person well." This was a great prayer because I thought all I could do was hope that someday doctors might find a new drug to stop the seizures.

The whole idea of being healed was music to my soul. I never had looked at the fact I had already been healed of seizures without use of drugs and encephalitis, which were miracles in themselves. I do not remember my parents talking directly to me telling me I had been miraculously healed. In Isaiah 53:5, it says, "Christ was pierced for our transgressions, He was crushed for our iniquities . . . by His wounds we are healed." I could cling to this verse because it gave me hope.

After being invited back to other Sunday night services, the members got to know me better. Certain couples always picked me up and made sure Roger had no reason to worry about arranging transportation or my safety. They had asked me why I did not drive, so I shared parts of my past. Roger saw peace in me each time I came home and joy in my once sad spirit. I really looked forward to worship and being at my new church with friends who loved me unconditionally.

It had been over five years since the drive in the river, and seizures were still uncontrolled. Anointing oil and prayer could be my key to victory. I needed faith to believe that God would let it happen. This church was full of good news for me. In Hebrews 11:6, it says, "Without faith it is impossible to please God because anyone who comes to Him must believe He exists, and that He rewards them who diligently seek Him."

After being anointed the first time, an older lady came up to me and asked if she could pray for me. I told her I had uncontrolled seizures. Surprising to me was that she had also experienced seizures. I was always shocked to learn that I wasn't the only person in the world experiencing seizures. She gave me her telephone number and I called her daily. I finally had someone I could relate to, which was a blessing for me. She handled it all with a different attitude than mine. She answered her phone saying, "Jesus loves you," not the normal "hello."

I had no education on anything concerning the Bible. My mind was open to new teachings and I inhaled every minute at church on Sunday nights. People were gifts to me for I found wonderful friends who cared about me, took me shopping or to their homes to spend time with them. I was not lonely anymore. Phone calls were healing and friends encouraged me to keep believing and trusting God.

I knew certain verses that spoke directly to my needs. Philippians 4:13 was now stamped on my forehead from memory, in just a few months, "I can do everything through Him who gives me strength". I also knew the verse from Nehemiah 8:10 stating, "Do not grieve, but know that the joy of the Lord is your strength." I was going to need lots of strength to keep going and for my faith to blossom. I needed to trust in the Creator and become aware of His precious love for me.

I had no idea how long it would take before we'd find a drug that worked. God knew where I needed to be taught and He found this precious church just for me. I found the blessing to know Jesus and His love for me. Many scriptures were loaded with words to help me understand the meaning of healing and the many ways it was used throughout the Bible. My new life in Christ had started. The greatest gift I received was the salvation of my soul. Sunday nights were something I cherished.

The devil had played havoc on my emotions and self-worth through many nasty people I encountered and many hurtful situations I ran into. Stress had gone on a long time and God knew where I needed to be. I never had any religious upbringing, so whatever they taught, I inhaled all the way, no questions asked. I had no problem believing it, because it was the Word of God. This church was a great place to grow and to find out who you were in Christ. In 2 Corinthians 5:17 it states, "If anyone is in Christ, he is a new creation; the old had gone and the new has come."

Part Three

TRUSTING JESUS

Chapter 11

Jesus Becomes Real

My friend Cindy, who invited me to church, had a sister-in-law who lived three blocks from us. Lou Ann had four young children our kids' ages. I was lonely, so I walked over to her house every day after lunch, so our kids could have fun together. It was wonderful to have a good friend I could trust who cared about me and my children. There was never any formal invitation to come daily, but it became a special time away from our house.

Jesus was part of her makeup and that is what drew me to her. We were both young mothers and I now had someone who could listen to me as I asked many questions. She never told me, "Do not come. I am too busy." After many years, I do remember asking her when she saw us come daily through her yard, what she was thinking. She said, "I prayed a lot."

God was helping me start over this new life with Jesus. I could really be healed was all I could think about. I do remember watching people raising their hands in worship and thinking to myself, "Why should I do that?" It did not make sense to me because I had active seizures. I guess my thought patterns were mixed up, for I felt it would be easy to praise the Lord if I were healthy like the rest of the group. No one else had any problems.

I was told many times how amazing it was that I was still alive. I have no memory about my family telling me about God and how He kept me alive to enjoy a beautiful life. I never really thought deeply about it. God had a destiny for me. His goodness for my life was continually brought out to me in this new church. Without Jesus on my side, where would I be? Looking at my possible death experiences, I began to see clearly, that I had reasons to be praising God. In 1 Thessalonians 5:18, it states, "Give thanks in all circumstances, for this is God's will for you in Christ Jesus."

When we stop thanking Him, we take ourselves out of His perfect will for our lives. I learned God desired to hear praise from me while in the fiery furnace, no matter what. Sometimes while in a trial, we can attach deals with Him, like "if you heal me or let me live, then I will praise you." While in the midst of striking fear, like an emergency room, what He'd love to hear from us is telling Him, "Jesus I love you."

He leaves heaven and rescues us. Each day God gave me was a precious gift. These trials that continued were making me stronger to be able to fight the next seeming disaster. I found every person goes through struggles of their own. Prayer warriors knew my needs and I was protected and covered by His blood more than I could imagine. I was now understanding the reasoning for lifting up holy hands in reverence to the Lord, giving Him glory for the great things He does.

But now I was ready to express my feelings, for I really did have many reasons to be thankful. I remember the first time I lifted my hands I received peace. After many weeks of singing praises, it became natural and was my deep desire to do it all the time. God waited until I was ready and blessings kept coming and have never stopped since my first visit to the small Pentecostal church in Wausau, Wis.

I guess our Lord knows whether or not we will persevere under pressure, being totally aware that victory can and will be ours. Someday we will receive the prize of sitting with Him in heaven for eternity. We must respond and do our part. He can take us into our trials, so we can make necessary decisions to rise above and overcome pressures. He also can allow "problems" to stay around without any apparent reasons. I guess if we were released from them quickly, we would just relax and feel we had arrived. No inner change could happen and we would rest without ever pressing toward the mark for the prize . . . becoming His bride! So things went slowly, but they needed to, and every day brought me closer to Jesus and the wait was good for me.

After my being at the new church a few years, I grew stronger daily in the Lord. The prideful young student pastor decided he wanted his own church. Many of my closest friends left with him. It crushed the senior pastor whom I loved very much. I knew in my heart where I needed to be and stay. I will never regret that decision. God had brought me there for a reason and I was developing into a mature Christian knowing what was best for me.

I would learn to live without my friends and keep my eyes focused on Jesus, not the situation at hand. All who did leave returned after finding they had made wrong decisions. My friendships never really ceased, for we chatted on phones and I saw them occasionally. Jesus became my best friend and I learned to depend on Him, not them.

A man in our church made and a Bible cover for me. He wrote the scripture I loved from 2 Corinthians 12: 9 and 10, "My grace is sufficient for you for. My power is made perfect in weakness . . . . I delight in weaknesses, in insults, in hardships, in persecutions, in difficulties. For when I am weak, then I am strong." The date engraved on the inside leather cover was 1982.

Chapter 12

Aglow International

Many of the women at this church were part of Aglow International, which is a transdenominational organization of Christian men and women in over 172 nations of the world. It is one of the largest international organizations of its kind. Aglow reaches individuals each month through local groups, which is the heart of this movement.

Small Bible group studies, care support, retreats and annual conferences make up the Aglow year. Two foundational pillars of Aglow are prayer and outreach. Members go out into communities in many directions: prisons, nursing homes, inner-city neighborhoods, mental institutions, single mother's groups, as well as to neighbors who may need a cup of tea and a chat with a friend.

Our Aglow group met monthly and I was invited to go and share in fellowshipping with all of them. Someone always picked me up, so Roger was never involved in my transportation needs. I had many friends in Aglow and church who I could lean on and be encouraged by, in everything that seemed distressing to me. Jesus knew I would need support and compassionate friends who really would be with me through many dangers, trials and snares, and without Aglow, I would have sunk many times.

Aglow became a major part of my life as I grew in The Lord. Its teachings and beliefs set me free of many strongholds I had going against me. Friends from Aglow encouraged me to write this book to uplift and give strength to hurting people. They became my hands and feet through fearful testing and were able to keep me floating above water and helped me stay alive. They spent hours with me in prayer and many came to keep me company when I was lonely and afraid.

I found I enjoyed national and international conferences with close Aglow friends whom I was blessed to share time with at the large meetings. For example, there were around 10,000 men and women at one conference in Orlando, Fla. They came to hear speakers and worship the Lord. The international conferences are awesome because most of the women from the 172 nations come in their native dress and carry their countries' flags in a long parade so all can see and greet them.

Most attendees speak fluent English, but there are interpreters in all the languages. The speakers are taped so messages can be shared when everyone returns home. Music is an important part of Aglow and it is inspiring and wonderful hearing spiritual music sung by hundreds and thousands of men and women. I also enjoyed meeting many wonderful people each time I go, and I came to look forward to seeing them again at another large meeting.

The conferences have become a time of visitation from the Lord, individually and corporately. It is during these times that Aglow members and guests catch visions from leaders and authors who come to speak and can become equipped to return as servant leaders in their communities. Aglow has taken a mandate to answer God's call to minister to the Muslims, while bringing awareness of the basic theological differences between Islam and Christianity.

Another mandate is to stand in loving support for Israel and the Jewish people, while helping to bring awareness to the Body of Christ, concerning God's plans and purposes for these people He calls, "the apple of His eye."

Aglow is part of me and I have been totally blessed by this movement. Israel is a major part of Aglow and over the years Roger and I have been blessed many times traveling there for missions work. God has led us exactly where He wants us. We are sincerely grateful to have been part of all these travel groups and have enjoyed walking where Jesus and his apostles walked and ministered to hurting people.

Chapter 13

Years with Children

Chris was now old enough to go to school for half-day kindergarten. Since I could not drive, he had to get on a school bus very early in the morning. I actually got teary when he got on the bus and waved good-bye for the first time. Things were easier now without Chris causing problems between the two of them. He seemed to start fights easily by taking things away to upset her.

Elizabeth and I kept busy ourselves cooking, reading together, making crafts and enjoying quiet time. I made clothes for her dolls and both of us. She loved playing with all her dolls and got along well playing by herself. We had time for walks and biking until late fall, when the snow came that trapped us inside. We waited for rides to shop and to go to doctor appointments for blood levels of various drugs when Roger got home from work. Not very exciting for anyone, but it was part of life in that season

We were glad when snow melted and we could

get outside again for fun. Summers went quickly because of yard work, planting flowers or vegetables, and enjoying fresh clean air while bike riding and long walks. Roger always planned wonderful camping trips in different areas north of us and as the kids got older, we camped out of state.

There were magnificent bike trails and lakes for swimming and boating. We set up a large canvas tent near the picnic tables and cooked most meals there for a week or two. We met many out of state residents who became good friends as we shared life stories. We got a canoe for shallow river rides going long ways and a speed boat for water skiing and scouting out new areas. We were always having fun just being together.

While raising the children. I was told by many friends that I seemed to be "not quite there," because of overdoses of drugs swimming around in my system. My body had no alternative but to adjust to higher levels of medications, which was the treatment at that time. Although many memories of those trying years are not clear in my mind, I always knew inside that Jesus protected me through it all. I do have many lovely thoughts about raising kids and the fun that was involved.

Chapter 14

Coping with Seizures

I had a friend from the epilepsy support group named Terri. She also had complex partial seizures like I was experiencing. She had a ride to our home to visit and meet our cat whom everybody loved to see. Roger happened to arrive home while she was there having a seizure. She started digging around in her purse and got up quickly, started walking around in circles and went into the bathroom and sat back down again.

It was amazing to see this, because Roger told me that it was exactly what I did during my seizures. So now I was able to see firsthand what people witnessed as I had a seizure. Truly amazing that I never hurt myself badly, nor did Terri. She lived by herself and hated life, and within a few months of her visit, I was told she committed suicide as many victims do.

Aglow girls were special caregivers while Roger was at work. Bible studies at church on Wednesday mornings and other prayer groups at homes nearby invited me to join them. I have no recollections about the studies or who was in them. I blacked out and fell wherever I was, and was protected and caught while falling. While Roger was at work, God knew just who I needed to surround and care for me with love 24/7. I have seen falls from other victims, which is hurtful to see.

Our family kept fighting this uphill battle to stop the seizures. We made the best of it and lived one day at a time. Doctors had their hands up as to how to handle the seizure patterns. They were totally dumbfounded and had no ideas how to end the activity. All I could do was pop pills daily, but to no avail.

Our children stayed home and entertained themselves and occasionally a friend was able to get to our house. Chris rode his bike everywhere which helped him socialize. School provided many sports activities, but our kids never enjoyed fun after-school games with their friends, because Mom couldn't pick them up after school and Roger got home after five.

Many people have asked me what the most difficult part of waiting for healing was. Many assumed it was dealing with side effects of drugs. They were wrong. The seizures themselves never bothered me because I never knew when one was about to or had happened. The loss of independence and needing to ask for rides was horrible. Just hearing Roger say he'd be out of town on business was terrible, for I knew transportation would now be gone. If emergencies happened, finding someone was not easy.

When I'd ask people who didn't know me for a ride, the first thing they'd say in a friendly way, "Get a license; it is easy to drive." When I told them I had seizures, I frequently never saw them again. People were fearful while watching a seizure and had no idea what to do. I got tired of hearing excuses and their reactions to my needs, so I quit asking for rides. It was kind of a "give up and sink" attitude. And some people were just plain mean. Thankfully, Jesus had found a caring church family for me who encouraged me to fight on. That was what kept me treading water and doing a somersault once in a while just to stay afloat.

One day a woman named Laura called and told me a friend had suggested she call me because she knew I loved to swim. Laura said she'd take me to the same healthcare pool that I had used to bring Lori "back to life." She wanted to meet me and take me to the pool. I was elated. I loved swimming laps. The warm water relaxed my muscles which made it hard to continue going long distances. Six women, 20 years older than I was, befriended me and were caregivers as I swam, because a seizure could happen anytime.

Lifeguards were warned, too, but they were socializing and were not as attentive as they should have been. Doing a water ballet activity, I had a seizure. Thankfully, a man in a dress suit was walking in the pool area, saw me under water, jumped in and rescued me. I was hospitalized overnight. The lifeguards were fired because of their neglect. They were angry at me and I felt guilty. But I had done nothing wrong. It was a healthcare pool. The new lifeguards were told they could not leave their chairs while I swam. The devil was working overtime trying to kill me but drowning was not in God's book for my destiny.

I inwardly realized after years of seizures since the initial drive in the river, I should just accept not driving again. I had to stop telling God what I wanted and how He should do it. I had to let go of my life and start praying for others. I had been blessed to be alive and healthy and strong. Seizures should not dictate my being. I never was institutionalized like the doctors had planned. I was happily married with two healthy kids. Why was I always wanting more? Perhaps I was very selfish.

I needed to learn patience, rid myself of anger or self-pity, and stop complaining or grumbling. Quite a large pill to swallow. If I wanted freedom, testing would be part of the discipline. Humility says God knows best and will not be late. When the time is right, He will exalt and lift us up. When we let go, dying to self can happen. However, waiting on God becomes quite a challenge.

Was I ready for this challenge? I knew there were drug studies but nothing new on the market. I desperately put my hands up and said, "I want Your will to be done, and I surrender my life totally and completely to You." Fighting for my healing was plain ridiculous, because He makes the rules.

Chapter 15

Open Door to Healing

It was now in the early 1990's and seizures continued. A problem had arisen because I was now seeing "two" of everything on television. I had never shared this concern, because I didn't think it mattered. I asked Roger while watching a golf tournament, "Why am I seeing double of everything on the screen?" He looked at me saying, "You're kidding, right?"

That did it. We decided to get a second opinion from the nearby Marshfield Clinic, which is affiliated with the famous Mayo Clinic in Rochester, Minn., that specializes in seizures disorders and brain injuries. My proud neurologist in Wausau wouldn't release records they needed, so we went to our family physician, Dr. North, who did it immediately.

I had an appointment within a few days with the head neurologist in the department. He was a brilliant doctor who ordered blood work, an EEG and other necessary tests to make an analysis. While looking into my eyes carefully, he calmly said, "There would be no need for further testing." He stated clearly that the tests showed at least "a triple overdose."

He was amazed that I could walk a straight line. It could take about a year to rid my body of the overdose, because it had to be done gradually. I could not just stop taking it, for that would cause severe problems.

While waiting that year for excessive amounts of drugs to rid my system, we had also been told too many drugs could increase the frequency of seizure problems. We were just thrilled to have taken that step of faith in finding a specialist who had new ideas to help us walk up this mountain and get the answers on how to move on to a victory.

Since over the years I had tried all the drugs on the market, we decided to see if I'd qualify to be in a drug study. I would love the independence and freedom. The study involved signing paperwork stating I could not sue if damages were done to me physically or mentally while on the study. I really believed it could work and signed my life away.

There had not been any success stories with any new drug, but maybe I might be the first one. To be qualified, I had to have had at least six seizures each month, which we knew was likely. But we didn't know for sure because I personally couldn't tell if I had one or not. Sometimes I could tell by new bumps or bruises or the family or friends would witness one. Nevertheless, I was admitted into the study.

A short time after taking the first pill, I knew this was not a placebo. My head felt spaced out and heavy and my legs became weak. The drug was powerful, but because I had a large frame, my body could handle it. It caused blurry and sometimes double vision. There were side-effects, but I just had to hang on. If I forgot a dose, I couldn't take more, because overdosing caused bad reactions. Brain surgery was not possible because my seizures came from both sides of my brain. Some friends I met at the support group had surgery because their seizures came from one side.

I was a fighter and going for the prize. I trusted God wanted me healed again like when I was 14 years old. I was ready to walk on water, believing God made this pill for me. Bad side effects happened with any drug, so why worry? There is no problem too big for God to handle. As seizures continued, my doctor increased drug amounts every three months, and seizure activity became less frequent which was exciting.

Roger lost many hours at work taking me to appointments and staying with me. A friend from college days lived near the clinic and offered to bring me back home after each appointment. After seeing the doctor, we enjoyed lunch and shopping together. This worked well. Another answer to prayer!

After six months, seizures seemed to cease during the day, but one seemed to occur quite frequently early before arising. It was disappointing but I was a fighter. On my own, I decided to try more drugs at bedtime and less during the day which worked well, so we had another victory!

I was my doctor' poster child, for this new drug had no success stories besides me. I was genuinely elated. God had blessed me with a "not-yet-FDA-approved drug," which I received free of charge for over 10 years. Once approved, the cost was very expensive so they invented a generic drug but it was not strong enough so I stayed on the initial drug.

Back in 1974, driving regulations were different than now in 1990. A friend helped me and it became easy for me. My independence, freedom and self-worth were restored and I felt blessed 100-fold. No more waiting or calling for rides. I was able to pick up others who had need, which lifted my spirit. I felt like an eagle soaring, and it was freedom I had longed for.

I am sure Roger was concerned more than I will ever know, but he was willing to let go and trust I would be all right. This drug was a gift made from God. My other drug I had taken for years had adverse side-effects, and the doctor said I could eventually get off it and take more of the new drug.

My faith continued to soar as I became more mature in Christ. I read His word on healing and enjoyed many deep Bible studies while sharing His word with others. Hearing evangelists and going to many Aglow conferences nationwide and all over our state, people continued to pray for my healing. Many heard my testimony and were amazed at all the miracles God had performed, which elevated my faith. Believing and knowing I was healed of seizures without drugs before, why not again?

I did have blurred vision and spaced out feelings occasionally, which I learned to accept. The older drug caused my emotions to run wild, especially when I was tired, which I put up with, but sometimes my reactions became embarrassing to me. My friends understood me while caring for my needs for many years.

It never bothered them, but I had no control when this happened. Inwardly I really believed drugs could be ruled out and it would be an awesome testimony for God's glory for people to see He heals even in the 20th century! What a fabulous destiny would be mine just sharing His love with hurting people. I was becoming more bold and strong in faith and my self-confidence soared.

I began getting truths out of proportion, and was not really thinking clearly about the pros and cons of the actual safety of my excitement and reasoning as I was making decisions. There were many inside feelings in me that became confused and distorted and was proving to be negative and not good for me. I kept going forward, feeling nothing could stop me and my new faith. I was walking on water versus drowning as before.

Part Four

TRIALS CONTINUE

Chapter 16

Time for Learning

Sometimes when you ask for more fruit, you may be given serious testing to help you grow to be more like Him. These were good things to ask for, but we are rarely prepared as to ways God would answer them. We all like comfort zones and being free of stress and pain.

I wanted to be healed and was looking forward to having God reveal Himself to me. I prayed, "Show me your glory. I've got to see you. I want to know you more." So many Biblical verses were continually put to music, which made it very easy to learn scripture and sing a tune, telling Jesus how you felt and you much you loved Him.

His purpose in making you want to run to him is that you seek Him more deeply than you ever have in your whole life. This pursuit of God is what changes you. I actually heard pain is critical to success, and the enemy wants us to always to give up when any affliction is placed on us. All testimonies

71

start with pain and go to gain and then reigning with Jesus can happen.

I wanted to share my testimony so badly to give people hope. But God's timing was not there for me yet. Friends kept sharing these words for me, "When God is ready, it will happen." But waiting was never easy for me. Jeremiah 29:13 states, "You will seek Me and find Me when you seek me with all your heart." So I needed to grow in faith and trust. I could not get enough of His Word into my Spirit. There is a song saying, "Make me, mold me, fill me, use me . . . I give myself to You, the Master Potter."

I wrote a few short articles about my life's testimony and its miracles that have been published already. *Angels on Earth* and *Guideposts* said no, saying we have "too many stories like it." The answer they gave did not really make any sense to me. However, *Spirit Led Woman* magazine liked what I wrote. It is an international magazine, which I found was far more exciting.

The devil always had an agenda for me, which was trying to get me upset and lose patience with God, when it seemed in my mind that things looked black. He tried very hard to disorient me, as well as discourage me. I had to learn to hold on and thus be changed in the process. Things were going well and the devil gets upset when he sees anyone holding on and walking with righteous standards. He now saw a bold servant Jane, wanting to evangelize and save others to bring them to Jesus.

I had read a book by Tom Barnett called *There*

is a Miracle in Your House. On one page he had stated clearly that if you keep a vision for five years or more and do not give up, it will come to pass. Ever since I heard some stories about how sick I had been from family and friends and saw how God was there through it all, my vision was to tell the world. Habakkuk 2:3–4 says, "For the revelation awaits an appointed time, it speaks of the end and will not prove false. Though it linger, wait for it; it will certainly come and will not delay."

So I kept believing that God would let me speak for Him. I found that the more you desire to walk in Jesus' shoes, the more fires can burn. When you pray, "Lord change me," be prepared to suffer as He did for us. Greater faith happens when vessels are broken. God was going to do a shaking in me, for He is the Potter and I was the clay. He would be examining my heart and then bring on the fire to purify me, so I could be used for His glory.

What I was to remember through all of this was when I was being tested, Jesus was with me and I had to persevere and fight the fight that would be coming soon. I was to know that in the swirling waters and overwhelming high tides that could threaten to kill me, I would have the keep kicking and stay afloat. The Lord does not always calm the waters, keep floods from coming or put out fires. The seeming disaster won't destroy you and you can always walk on with hope. You will never walk alone (a favorite song with great words to hold onto).

Chapter 17

Whose Decision Was It?

My faith became stronger daily. I truly believed healing was on the doorstep. God had stopped the lengthy grand mal seizures of three months when I became conscious, without the use of drugs. Doctors realized they were not necessary and gave God the upper hand.

I assumed my motives and desires were right, even though my knowledge of the seriousness of my decision-making may not have been evident to me. I was being blind-folded by the devil. My nurse friends, doctors, family, church, Roger and I were all thrilled we found this miracle drug Lamictal, I had actually been healed with drugs, without severe side effects. Why was I not getting the point? I should have just left things as God wanted them, using His gift he gave me.

The devil is the father of lies and enjoys whitewashing my mind into trying another plan he was creating. I was oblivious to it all. God totally blessed me and I seemed to want to do my own thing. I seemed to think and felt strongly, that God was going to heal me again without the use of drugs. I really believed it was His plan and not mine. My plan seemed to be based on faith and trust (never putting two and two together.)

Now looking back, I really cannot imagine I would have even believed such a stupid thing. I truly knew in my heart that God does heal without drugs, but was this really His plan? I was taking so many scriptures out of context, reading into them as to what I thought they meant. I felt if God had done it before in my life, he could do it again.

It would be only for His glory. I was not doing this for my pride, thinking that I was just so special. I thought only about how great it would be telling others the seizures were healed by His stripes and drugs were not always the necessary healing aids. I knew sharing this testimony would open eyes to see it can still happen in the 20th century. I wanted to be used by Him so people would believe in miracles again.

Truly, my only incentive was to give God glory. I think God knew that. However, my plans were not His, and I was going to learn a very hard lesson from all of this.

Many of my friends told me it was not a good idea to stop taking drugs. I should have listened to them. A friend asked me for a ride to Marshfield, so I thought I might have a chance to ask my doctor about stopping drugs. He might give me a thumb's up and be aware of my plan. I dropped her off for her appointment and amazingly walked right into Dr. Ruggles in the lobby. I told him my old drug was awful and I wanted to get off of it. He told me to add more of the victory drug Lamictal, and then stop the other one. I had his permission. Now the playing pieces of my puzzle were good.

I wanted to change one major rule, for my plan was no drugs at all. The doctor never heard that part of my plan. I cannot believe I actually wasn't afraid to try stopping drugs completely. When I got home, I flushed down the toilet all the bad side-effect drug. It was not a slow process at all. I felt fine and told Roger I hated the emotional tears it brought. He said he was fine with my stopping Tegretol, but stay on new one as the doctor told me. I was strong-willed and wanted my plan, because I knew it would work. But it was a pretty senseless idea.

My mind was made up and feelings of victory were all I thought about. In my heart I trusted this would work. I shared with a few people how excited I was, but I am sure they were praying inwardly all the time, for me not to do it. They were hoping I would see the light and stop the nonsense. My mind was washed of any truths of concerning how ridiculous this idea was.

In 1962 God did the miracle. I was now set and ready to show everyone He still could do it. To this day, why or where these ideas came from is beyond me. The mind can really get trouble brewing fast. Fear was not there and seizures were not happening, as far as I knew. My plan just continued on like clockwork.

The reality of its possible outcome never dawned on me. I was totally blind to the repercussions as to how it would affect everyone. I stopped taking the new drug totally and was drug free and inwardly felt relieved and at peace. I was excited. My faith seemed whole and I knew God could do anything. I just had a few major pieces of the puzzle out of place. I never heard God speak to me, telling me that this was His plan. It was what Jane wanted to do.

I was at church after four months now without drugs in my system. There was an evening Bible study with the ladies, and I had a seizure while helping lead worship. I fell flat down and broke my forearm. My arm was very sore surrounding the fracture, because skin was torn inwardly and many nerve cells were damaged.

A friend had brought me into the sanctuary and told me about the seizure. I had no idea why my arm hurt badly. I just thought this was a scare tactic the devil threw at me and to not be afraid. Totally oblivious to reality and wisdom. God was being gracious to me, letting me know my plan was a bad idea, but I ignored this warning of mercy. I still believed drugs were unnecessary. Unreal. I had one track mind and it was de-railed. I did have very strong faith, but what I was believing was a lie of the enemy.

I was walking blind on water, totally unaware my faith would soon disappear. I was standing on Philippians 1:6 verse stating, "He who began a good work in you, will be faithful to complete it in you." His work would be done in me and I was ready to tell the world God heals in the 1990s. As far as I was concerned, the healing was there and my testimony was finished. Nehemiah 8:10 states, "Do not grieve, for the joy of the Lord is your strength." I brought joy to others by loving and sharing time with them. I met many at the epilepsy support group who needed hope, for a drug or miracle themselves. Seeing my victory would give them encouragement.

There was a revival at our church during my getting "free without drugs in me" period. They sang beautiful songs of praise and worship. I was spending more time with God and drawing closer to Him daily. I wanted to be used by God and to be pure and righteous in His eyes, and also a delight to Him.

I had been up at my friend Marilyn's house all afternoon, and I was on my way home to make dinner. It had been about five months with no drugs in me. Many were praying for me, and Roger was waiting for something to happen, as he now knew I was on nothing to stop seizures. He didn't agree with me. I was just blind to any dangers involved. I was singing along with my CD's blaring, as I was praising the Lord. My brain seemed free without drugs.

Chapter 18

A Disaster Hits

Then it happened. I had a seizure while I driving at 65 m.p.h. When I was about to turn off at our exit, my body collapsed and fell forward, as it had happened at the riverside back in 1974. Witnesses later told me my car went down into a deep ditch and stopped. It was when I fell forward, jerking my body again, that my foot hit the accelerator and the car zoomed up a steep embankment quickly. It smashed into a bunch of birch trees at the top of the hill.

When I was slowly awakening, I was sitting on the hillside in the deep grass in total confusion. I had no idea what had just happened. I saw a fire engine and ambulance at the bottom of the hill and two men running up towards me with a gurney. I remember telling them I was not going to any "dumb" hospital and that I was fine. I signed papers refusing to go to the hospital.

There were people slowly walking up the hill

asking softly, "Are you all right? Do not move." I turned, looking back up the hill from where I was sitting. I saw my 1996 purple Saturn smashed. Reality was now becoming the main focus. My mind was clearer, now that the seizure was over. I had experienced a severe car accident and I had no scratches, bruises or blood anywhere on me. I stood up, brushed the dust and grass off and walked down the hill to the police car for them to take me home so I could make dinner.

I do remember hearing someone saying aloud, "She has someone who really cares about her." I had just bought a bumper sticker the night before the accident saying, "Jesus loves you." There was a reason I had a smile all over my face. God had sent His angels once again to protect me from harm. Why? That was the big question. I certainly did not merit this gift, considering I knew I should never have gone off my drugs.

The light was finally dawning. I could have been killed and taken to heaven. Or I could have killed other people! I guess God wanted me to stay down here on earth awhile longer. The car doors were still locked and the windshield was severely cracked. But there had been no one up there when the car smashed into the trees to try to help me get me out. But God made sure I was whole and unharmed.

What greater love was this that He would bless and save me, though I had never listened to wisdom from my friends. His love and compassion are truly amazing. I did not deserve to be rescued, considering I had been warned to stay on drugs. I had acted shamefully and needed some severe discipline. The possibility of ever finding the correct amount of drugs that had been established over many years, would not be an easy task for the doctors. It would be a very steep hill to climb.

Would God even want to give me another chance for healing after all my game playing? God's decision was in control. I did learn my lesson this time the hard way. You cannot look back and say, "I should have, could have." I did deeply regret neglecting good advice from all who shared and went overboard praying for me. I just didn't get it. I was an accident waiting to happen. It was totally amazing I actually lasted five months without drugs in me and seizure free.

The devil did not get his way. The idea that another miracle had just occurred was too much for him. This would be another uphill battle for me and a very humbling experience. I had been very wrong in doing my will and I had to apologize to my husband, friends and the doctor. I truly do not remember anyone shaking their finger at me saying, "I told you so," or calling me stupid for doing such a dumb thing.

I felt bad enough and regretted everything. I had really hurt Roger and felt worse about that more than anything else. He had come home that night after the police had dropped me off and calmly asked, "Where is your car?" When I told him, he was in shock, hugging me but not angry or yelling at me. He was grateful I was still alive.

So I had to start all over, for the seizures were happening, and you cannot just start over on 1,100 milligrams of drugs overnight. This would be a long drawn-out battle and no one really knew if success would even be an option. It was all in God's Hands. I was very depressed and I needed rides again. My kids took me to the grocery store or appointments while Roger was at work. Everything was backwards and it was all my fault. Everyone knew I was aching inside and all concerned were standing with me through all the healing process.

I carefully read scriptures from Psalm 71:20, "Though you have made me see troubles, many and bitter, you will restore my life again," and in verse 21, "You will increase my honor and comfort me once again." Anything I read gave me hope.

Psalm 91:9–11 states, "If you make the Most High your dwelling . . . , then no harm shall befall you, no disaster will come near your tent. For He will command his angels concerning you to guard you in all your ways." Verse 14–15 continues, "Because he loves me, I will rescue him; I will protect him, for he acknowledges my name . . . I will be with him in trouble, I will deliver him and honor him." I believe angels rescued me. How else did I get out of the car?

I had to trust I would see light at the end of the

tunnel...although things seemed pretty black and fear kept haunting me with nasty thoughts from the devil. He did want me to sink and would try anything to help me go under water and drown. I had to realize what God was capable of, knowing full well He loved me. It was sad to say I really questioned myself if drugs would work again.

Praise and worship elated me as I danced with my banner flying. It was disappointing when I did fall, and found myself awaking in someone's arms, because I then knew more drugs would be needed.

After a few months my body handled drug increases better, causing less seizures to occur. I was told we all need the heat of pressure and problems to grow in our faith. I needed endurance, patience, and the ability to stand fast. Endurance has to do with how much iron there is in a person. We never know what kind of iron there is until pressure of life's circumstances bring us up to a moment of decision, to choose to sink or swim.

God allows the devil to sift us "like wheat." God knows we have "wheat" inside to be threshed out. I needed to be cleansed of pride to produce meekness in my life. It did feel terrible, but God caused it to work for good. Before God can use us, we will pass through a time of threshing. I would be getting more discipline in humility.

The key to overcoming the devil is being humbled by God. The devil hates it because it is the surrender of the soul to God and he is terrified of Jesus. My desire to tell everyone that God heals without drugs was foolish pride. How a mind can get so confused with reality is when the devil gets his foot in the door. The devil tried to pull me away from God. But it drew me closer to Him. The Father's goal was to transform my life into the beautiful nature of His Son.

I had to learn to forgive myself, which I found to be very difficult. How I could have been so stupid to actually stop drugs was beyond me. I needed my eyes focused only on Him, not me. It was after three months of no seizures and I would be able to drive again. So we waited eagerly for three months to pass and a seizure always seemed to happen.

This condition continued for over a year. I was ready to pull the plug but I just couldn't do it because I had come too far to just give up. I kept singing praises, despite my frustration and disappointment. I trusted He would heal me to be a spokeswoman for Him sharing my testimony of His goodness. Caring friends blessed me with rides to appointments and Bible studies.

Even though it seemed I was always in the valley, which is a better place to grow, I was going to have to trust God for another mountaintop experience. Hebrews 12:5–6 states, "Do not make light of the Lord's discipline and do not lose heart when He rebukes you, because the Lord disciplines those He loves." This was good for me to read.

Job 5:17–18 states, "Blessed is the man whom

God corrects; so do not despise the discipline of the Almighty." Many people prayed for me and encouraged me to fight hard. God's view of this trial was different than mine. I wanted to please Jesus and I was told that God created a plan to revive and restore me.

When God takes us through Job's valley, He removes from us every ability to fight and thrust forward. God wants your pain to press you into His face that will produce change in you.

The time seemed endless while waiting for the correct amount of drugs to work. God had brought me through another almost death experience, and He wanted to see my victory. Most often those who walk through fire and deep water come out on top. I could be a testimony to encourage believers it is possible to be refined through suffering. For them to see a sufferer who survives by God's grace would be a positive witness giving them hope.

The timing is God's and the attitude is up to you. You can become angry or let go and accept responsibility. You can look down on problems or look up to Jesus and wait for His plan. God takes no pleasure watching human suffering. Isaiah 25:8 states, "The sovereign Lord will wipe away tears from all faces." No matter how many times you fail or how deep the water was that you fell in, His plan for your recovery is sure.

Even though the enemy and my mistakes seemed to have drained my strength, God's love was beyond my comprehension. No one overcomes by sitting down. Jesus already won the battle and we are declared winners working under His command. Although I did not feel like a conqueror right now, Jesus had already passed the baton to me. John 20:21 states, "As the Father has sent me, I am sending you."

I was in a battlefield standing on faith. He allowed this because the Spirit was working inwardly in me and Christ's glory was being formed for all eternity. God was in control. He was allowing tribulation and I had to endure what was dealt to me. God was in the process of conforming me to the image of His son.

I was told to rejoice in pain, knowing God would reverse the situation and use it to re-commission me. They told me I would re-emerge stronger than ever and the devil would see all his work backfire. That sounded lovely to me. I needed to stay floating in the rough turbulent water, knowing I would not have to tread water forever. Psalm 118:7 states, "I shall not die but live and declare the works of the Lord."

There are two ways to view chastening from God, either as punishment or promotion. God does allow His followers to serve as examples for everyone. Those who have suffered and walked through pain can be anointed to speak and help hurting people. Their gifts are empathy and compassion.

Chapter 19

Reaching Out in Love

I wondered what God would do while I watched the clock tick by that full year. It was touch and go many days, but I knew one thing for sure: I would never get off drugs on my own or play games with my body or God. I found out the hard way and the discipline hurt, but looking back, it was good for me.

All my close friends were now working part-time. I had no desire to use my education degree to teach or substitute teach. I tried subbing at the pre-school at church, but the kids ran the show. Children were now just plain nasty with no respect for subs anymore. So I decided to see if there was some sort of job like my friend Marilyn had with helping elderly people.

Elderly folks shared compassion and grace to hurting people. I had received this gift from them that I now could share with others. Many were best friends who had walked the walk through hardships I encountered. Their love kept me strong. They were part of Bible studies and prayer group and blessed me with transportation whenever I needed it. I was cared for with love and never had to give anything in return. This love can rub off on you easily

I had been blessed with a servants' heart. Working with disabled and handicapped people is very special and dear to me. For that type person was the former me, for most of my life.

Marilyn had heard about me, because of her need to find a specialist in neurology. She had seizures, but hers could be stopped with surgery and drugs could then be forgotten. I met and had lunch with her and got an appointment with my doctor to see if he had ideas to get her seizure free. He set her up with a surgeon so now she is independent and seizure-free. It felt great to help her, like I had helped Lori. We gave hope to hurting people to have vision to see they had a chance. We were living, breathing testimonies, who had been blessed with healing victories. We held their hands and shared long hours with them.

There was a group that did respite care for in-home needs. Although I had no CNA degree, I could do the job well. I traveled all over the Wausau area to different homes with elderly who needed extra care. I did cleaning, cooking, shopping and laundry, which was easy for me. I had done that kind of work many years in our house. It was exciting for me to be part of the work-force.

When you have a handicap, I had always assumed you were just plain unemployable. Many people always had asked why I did not work. This caregiver job I now had brought on a new sense of self-worth.

I made friends easily with the elderly. I listened to them compassionately and helped with their needs. Once in a while, my emotions took over, so I handled things in a "non-professional" way. I never hurt anyone and always finished jobs on good terms, but my employers chose to find another more qualified CNA to replace me. It hurt since I had done nothing to harm anyone.

Another care group hired me right away and I continued to help anyone who had a need. The group loved my creativity and ideas I shared with others. I drove clients to appointments or just got them out of their house. Problems arose that I was unaware of, so I was let go again. I was then hired by a single elderly woman. She had laundry, cats and many household chores to keep me quite busy. After being with her over six months, her niece in town needed a job, so my job was now hers.

I cared for elderly at Hospice houses or the hospital after completing many hours of classes. I found that it was very rewarding. I enjoyed working in the hospital proper, not in individual homes. After many months of sharing in their sorrows and grieving with them, there seemed to be something missing. The reason then became apparent. I could not relate my life experiences, because I had never experienced death of a close family member. So I decided to leave Hospice on good terms.

Working with elderly was good experience. I was being prepared by God, for my Mom when she moved from Florida back to Wisconsin. It was disappointing to be fired from jobs for no apparent reason, but it was great experience so I could help my Mom.

Chapter 20

Closer to My Parents

My Mom and Dad moved from Wisconsin to Venice, Fla., because of his ill health. This move occurred while doctors continued looking for a drug that would stop my seizures. Dad needed a warmer humid climate for his breathing. Their move would make my ability to see them almost impossible because I could not travel alone.

With Roger's work schedule and kids in school, summer was the only time we could go together. When my brother visited them in Florida, he called and we enjoyed listening to what was going on in their lives. It was not the same as being there. My Mom was the spokesperson, since Dad couldn't speak with volume, so he never was able let himself be known.

Their lives went on for many years in Florida and did quite well on their own. They had many friends and enjoyed socializing. Dad played golf daily and Mom painted, sold her art work, and enjoyed bridge clubs. They enjoyed restaurants near the water or downtown. We loved coming to visit them in the summer, though it was quite warm and humid.

I did not know Mom well to discuss deep thoughts, or understand Dad's health problems, so we assumed all was well. We called weekly and they let us know they were fine and immediately changed the topic of conversation wondering how we were. Mom did not tell us the truth.

A severe cancer problem began again for Dad. It now returned at the base of his tongue. He breathed from the stoma in his neck, so no one had any idea there was a blockage. A tongue-bi-section would now eliminate his ability to vocally enunciate words to speak. He refused stomach tube feeding, and liquid Ensure with frozen yogurt was the only "staple" he could ingest. He needed liquid so his esophagus wouldn't dry out. Mom never made sure the glass was finished, which was dangerous. She wanted to move to an assisted-living facility or have help come in their home. He said no, so everything was on Mom's plate. She was a saint.

One day we got an urgent call from Mom, knowing Dad's health was on the line. We knew she desperately needed us and was relieved from severe stress when we arrived. He was 90% dehydrated, gasping for air. His esophagus did close from having very little liquids in it for a long time. They both were struggling to make it through each day and she kept it all to herself. He was admitted to the hospital and moved into the nursing home when his liquids returned to his system. Mom had no choice but to move into the assisted living area near-by, which upset her. After about a month, Dad was taken home to be with the Lord.

She was now in Florida alone but we needed her in Wisconsin near us. So my brother Tom and I decided to move her as soon as possible. I was excited because I never had memories of quality time with Mom. I was always told by her friends what a fun and silly personality she had and she made them all laugh. She had taken care of me and now the tables were turned. It was my joy to accept the responsibility as her caregiver.

In 2002 Roger and I found a great assisted living facility that let her keep both cats. Tom and I flew to Florida bringing Mom to Wausau close to our home. She liked her new place but she insisted we go out for lunch daily and then go shopping to buy clothes for both of us. She seemed lonely and I now had time to enjoy time with her. Unfortunately, she seemed to need a hot fudge sundae after every lunch so we had extended time together. I consumed lots of iced tea to fill me up, so I could watch her eat most of it but yet control my weight gain.

I loved the responsibly and challenge of caring and sharing concerns of her needs with my brother on the phone. We made decisions together about her care. It made me feel important and useful. Mom got to know the new me as we spent quality time together. Tom came to visit a few times a year and he stayed at our house, which was a good time for me to get to know him better. I never knew Tom well because he lived so far away for many years. He was a hospital administrator in California and I believe he chose that field because of his time and experiences with both me and Dad's illnesses and his compassionate spirit.

Part Five

ACCEPTING CHALLENGES

Chapter 21

A New Physical Challenge

Mom and I enjoyed time together, but her health declined as years went by. She developed an anxiety problem, so she was moved to a smaller facility that gave her more care. The room was smaller and she could only keep one cat. Roger and I took her out for many lunches, dinners and shopping to get her away from the facility.

The residents there were anti-social and she was depressed. She slept too much because they overdosed her to keep her from yelling when she wanted attention. Drugs were damaging her joyful spirit. We bought a lightweight wheelchair so we could take her out for lunches and now doctor visits, which made it difficult for us to go out as often. We wanted her happy and to feel loved.

She had deep concerns for me emotionally and physically, as mothers often do. She and my friends asked why I limped or if I was in pain while walking. One leg was longer, so it seemed obvious to me that it was the reason. I decided to see an orthopedic doctor at the nearby clinic to get an answer from an expert.

X-rays showed my hip bones were disintegrating. To my surprise and horror, he said a hip replacement would be necessary. I was only 58, which seemed ridiculous because I was so active. He told me the limp would be gone by using a longer pin in the thigh bone to correct it. I had pain in the groin area, where hip sockets are located. I thought my swim fins had stretched my muscles in that area, which had caused the pain. Not so. This would be major surgery.

This young surgeon was a specialist in hip revisions and used a new technique. The incision was four inches that would heal more quickly than the older nine inch kind. The sockets were made by Johnson & Johnson, metal on metal and estimated to last 20 years. I was scheduled for surgery soon after seeing him and excited about having no more pain while walking.

It was a deep cut right through the muscle. I could not exercise or bend over about three months while the incision healed, for the hip socket could be displaced. The surgery went well and I was out of bed and walking somewhat in pain the next day. I used a walker and a grabber to go anywhere or pick up anything. Because of no pain anymore, it was easy to forget that surgery had occurred and rehab was unnecessary. I was told that my age and being physically fit helped with healing and a speedy recovery.

God directed the surgeons' hands and a victory was mine. I couldn't drive for a few months which reminded me of the past and needing rides. Roger put in double time at home and work. I needed help getting dressed and in the shower. Once I did lose my balance getting up too quickly. It was really scary. X-rays showed everything was still in place. I would need antibiotics for safety. If infection got into my system and affected the metal area, the new sockets would be damaged and surgery would be needed again.

Fear popped into my mind after almost falling. I was told I should monitor my thoughts, for they were the enemy's playground. The devil kept saying I could be handicapped for the rest of my life. However, I would find out within a few years that the doctor had not succeeded in leveling my legs, which would cause future problems. He suggested a shoe lift.

I wanted my victory. I was claiming no more hip problems. The devil always had a plan to drive fear and doubt into my whole being. He did not want any more of my testimonies of healing to be heard by anyone, anywhere. I was born a fighter. I needed to continue to swim fast and get a blue ribbon for completing the race.

After three months of waiting for the deep incisions to heal, I was now free again to go ahead with plans God had for me. One day a friend from Aglow asked me to join her in Israel while visiting a friend who was a missionary in Haifa. I decided to go. I flew stand-by and although it was Passover and flights were full, God opened up a flight on a larger plane than initially planned for us. He always has a perfect way for His children.

I was given a choice after arriving. I could sit in her apartment overlooking the beautiful Mediterranean Sea from 16 floors up or walk with them all over town as missionaries. I chose to go with them and forget about the recent hip surgery. But it was a challenge, since we were walking a lot, climbing stairs and occasionally jumping on a bus.

We traveled all over Haifa, delivering Bibles, books, and food to the Israeli people. We enjoyed reaching out to them with the Good News. By choosing exercise, my legs became stronger and more muscular. It was greater therapy than anyone could have received at rehab. God had brought me to Israel to strengthen me, give me the ability to minister to hurting people, and focus my eyes on others rather than myself.

Chapter 22

How Much More, God?

In June 2007 another major storm was beginning to brew, something I had never dreamed could happen. I already had my testimony ready to share, my destiny figured out and how God was going to use me for His glory, by sharing my blessings I had received. He just had to be finished with my "disasters." He wouldn't allow anything more to happen to me. I had gone through enough health issues.

Trials were in intended by God to teach wisdom. There would be a purpose for this very deep valley. Through His grace it is possible to uncover purpose in tragedy. Sometimes when we come to Him with struggles, He can turn sadness into joy with no effort on our part. You have to be able to understand that God can produce more fruit in longer trials, than if you received instant relief. Reasons for tragedy can be to give God glory. When you persevere in His fire, you can gain great boldness.

The Apostle Paul did not enjoy the act of suffering,

but he learned how to react correctly. If it looked like he was going to die, he rejoiced knowing he would be with Jesus soon. Philippians 1:23 states, "I desire to depart and be with Christ which is better by far, but it is more necessary for you that I remain in the body." I wanted to depart and saw no reason to continue on with the sagas of life.

You will suffer in this life, but when people see you going through an earthly sadness with heavenly joy, God is glorified. God waits for us to righteously react to negative situations, before He changes any situation. With this future coming trial, God would be testing me. It could work for my good in the end, but in layman's terms, it would be "hell on earth." Could I handle this new bombshell?

I had the devil spewing lies at me all the time, and he delighted in my having pity parties and fretting unnecessarily. I could not help him by hating myself and worrying constantly. Any thoughts that make you feel you are unloved and a failure are not from God. The devil steals joy getting you to dwell on your weaknesses. God loves it when we resist the devil (that is what Jesus did). Christ draws near to us in the midst of our battle. You must look for him diligently.

God wants fighters. To be victorious, you cannot roll over and die. Jesus will help you overcome and bring out the best in you. I would need my swim fins back on again, and go for the race well equipped. I had a new hip now, so I had no excuses about exercise. I had to stay prepared and never give up.

The devil was about to create a nightmare that I had no choices in decision making. The rock was thrown and I just had to go forward, even if it meant continual floating with a life jacket.

I had known my Mom had had breast cancer, but that wasn't gong to happen to me. It was 2007 and I was 59 years old. I had mammograms yearly, and only once did I need a biopsy. It was a calcium deposit, so I was safe, although very frightened.

It was time for another mammogram and I was pleased to hear it was negative. But I continued my self-exams, and a few days later I felt a tiny "baby, pea-sized rock" on a lower rib, far down from the breast itself. It did cause questions because I felt it only lying down but standing while showering, it was gone. This "rock" did not go away like I hoped it would. I decided to see a doctor, but fear caused me to want to run away from the truth. I reasoned it was not "on" the breast area and it was tiny, and lumps were big and easy to see. The mammogram had shown nothing, so why should I be concerned?

I went to a doctor and he ordered an MRI, another mammogram and a biopsy. The technicians expressed great concern looking at the results close up. The once peaceful atmosphere in the room disappeared and I was scared. My peace was totally gone. The next day I got "the call" and I drove there by myself. I was escorted to a small room and handed a box of Kleenex. They had found cancer and surgery had to be done shortly. I was in total shock.

In a panic mode, I paged our family doctor, David North, asking who he would recommend as a surgeon. He suggested Dr. Sally (known by her first name), whom had I seen before for other small day surgeries and consultations. She was very thorough and experienced. I got bold and I paged her at the hospital, to get things going faster. Somehow she remembered my name and answered the call. What a blessing, for she was leaving town later that afternoon, but squeezed us in before five o'clock. I guess being bold at times does help. I can't believe I was so gutsy.

She drew pictures where the incision would be, letting me know I would not lose my breast. She suggested I chat briefly with an oncologist prior to the surgery. I was not prepared for this verdict of cancer and still in disbelief. It all came too fast. A few days ago, I was fine and boom, the fire was lit.

While walking sheepishly down the corridor, reading the doctor's name on the door and seeing his grim face made me want to run and hide. But Dr. Sally let him know I'd be there. He let me know chemo was necessary for my cancer. I never sat down to talk because I had heard enough bad news already. I made up plans saying I had a lunch date and ran out of the clinic.

I called Roger and told him what the verdict was and he said clearly, "We will get through this together." I was stressed out and severe pressure surrounded me. I had to accept the gruesome cancer diagnosis and believe a good ending could occur. Jesus could heal me of this impending doom about to hit me smack in the face. Jesus was my way to cope, but I would find my faith quite shaky. I had to quit the blame game for not seeing the doctor right away. Anger and bitterness were right in the mix with all the other rocks thrown at me.

The storm had hit. Now what would I do? I had to act like Jesus did. He went to sleep. I had to be calm because Jesus said, "Peace be still" (Mark 4:39). He was still in me and I had to remember I was not alone in the boat on this coming storm. I could ride out the storm if I put my total trust in Him. It looked rough now, but I had to keep my eyes focused on Jesus. God knew what He was doing.

Cancer was now in my system. God had allowed it for some purpose, and I needed my blinders taken from my eyes. Dr. Sally explained the tumor was in the lower breast tissue and I had massive invasive Stage 3 cancer. My church family prayed that cancer cells were contained and had not spread. Dr. Sally said, "We won't know until we get in there."

The day arrived for surgery. Roger was told the longer it took, the more serious it was. He knew it was serious because he had waited three hours by himself. I came out of surgery with a drainage bag hanging out from under my armpit. The news would hit me in the head like a ton of bricks. Four lymph nodes had cancer so she removed 20 of them to be safe. I was not allowed to stay in the hospital overnight, because our insurance had pre-labeled it "day surgery."

I needed to put my life into the Lord's Hands, and stop worrying. Peace and contentment were available to me, but I had to first give it all to God. We are the clay that He molds to make us the way He wants us to be. I needed strong convictions inside of me, knowing I could stay afloat. Exodus 14:14 states, "The Lord will fight for you; you need only to be still."

The devil loves to torment women. He hates us and wants to take anything away that makes us who we are and what we look like. In Genesis 3, it shares that the offspring of the woman would eventually crush the serpent's head, a promise fulfilled in Christ's victory over the devil, a victory in which all believers share. I continually chanted in my soul, "He is under my feet, the devil is under my feet . . . Jesus is alive and the devil is a liar." I needed encouragement and singing praises always brought life back into me.

And more thought-provoking was this message in James 1:2–5. "Consider it pure joy when you face trials of many kinds because you know the testing of your faith develops perseverance." It was very difficult accepting this new cancer "trial testing" as joy. Death could be staring me in the face.

Chapter 23

Cancer Treatment Takes Its Toll

Since the cancer had spread into the lymph nodes, chemotherapy was the safest way cancer cells would be eliminated permanently. For recovery following surgery, I would have the choice to either be with a large group of patients who sat together chatting in chairs like a beauty parlor while poison entered their systems or go to the new hospital near our house which featured private rooms with a TV and a nice chair for my husband. I chose the private room.

Maybe a mastectomy was not necessary, but I knew every hair on my body would soon disappear. My hair had always been beautiful and made me feel special. After surgery my breast tissue was very sensitive because of raw skin covered by stitches. The drain tube was full all the time and was difficult to empty. My upper arm throbbed where lymph nodes were taken. My emotions were a mess. I had to recall the passage in Colossians 3:2, "Set your minds on things above, not on earthly things." I had to dwell and focus on Jesus, not postpartum surgery.

Trusting Jesus sounds an alarm bell off in hell. The devil hates Jesus and wants to ruin any relationship we have with Him. He will erect mountains of nasty conditions to help you know your life will soon be over. Cancer causes floods of doubt to rise quickly. The devil's agenda was to flatten me, making sure all I could see was black.

My church taught me a verse from James 5: 14, "Is any one of you sick? He should call the elders of the church to pray over him and anoint him with oil in the name of the Lord." Doctors never understood my faith, and were a form of dream killers. Prayer warriors encouraged me to know healing would come in His time and He knows our needs.

God despises sinful fear in us. We are blessed with a fiery guard of angels surrounding us. We have a God who puts Himself under oath to carry us through any disaster we face. I have heard that calamity is an instrument of God's love designed to purify and change us to become more like Jesus. Prayer chains went on 24/7, during this time of severe bodily havoc that had to continue if I chose to get well. I really felt their prayers. I had to pull through. Life was precious to me.

Isaiah 43:1–2 states, "Fear not, for I have redeemed you. I have summoned you by name; you are mine. When you pass through waters, I will be with you and when you pass through the rivers, they will not sweep over you. When you walk through the fire, you will not be burned." These verses spoke directly to me. He had never let me go, so what was I afraid of?

After the incisions healed, chemo was the next hurdle. Roger chose to take time off from work so he would be at my side during the procedure. Watching poison slowly drip into my once healthy body made me cringe. Where was wisdom found when there was now a need for poison to heal you?

I had to stay floating. I knew I was safe in His arms, but there is nasty voice that tells you to just drown and give up. The devil didn't like my boldness sharing love with others. Jesus was always my friend. I John 4:4 states, "You are from God and have overcome them, because the one who is in you is greater than the one who is in the world." Jesus was living in me and the worldly devil had no role in my life.

The staff in cancer care had great compassion and knew fear was evident. Only speculations were flowing through my mind, for all I heard prior to chemo was falsehood and testimonies of others who experienced symptoms which were mostly negative. My oncologist told us with Stage 3 cancer, eight sessions of treatments were necessary, with a month of radiation following chemo.

I could have said no to chemo and pulled the plug. I did love life, just not the present season. Chemotherapy did not involve pain. The procedure was two hours lying still. I never was nauseated which amazed everyone. I stood on Psalm 118: 17, "I will not die but live and will proclaim what the Lord has done." I knew healing scriptures, but I was not handling this fight like I thought I could.

So, I pondered His word in my heart, knowing this was discipline from Him, which would help me stand strong until the end. The battle that cancer would play in my life was unseen to me at this time.

Within 10 days, my hair was all over my pillow and while showering, on the tub floor. I screamed while watching clumps of hair fall out. I called my hair stylist and she heard panic in my voice and came after work. I wanted my head shaved to stop it. I knew my mind would have to let go and just accept my bald head. I remember telling Roger in tears, "I was ugly and life was not worth it." He asked me to not to think crazy thoughts, that he loved me with or without hair. Mom bought me a stylish wig that looked like my own haircut prior to it all falling out. Any outsider would never know it was a wig, but I surely did.

We went back every other week to a session of chemo for about three months. I felt like a sheep going to slaughter. I needed poison to rid bad cells, and my frail immune system disappeared. It would be a continual fight to stay strong and just to make it through another day. It was hard, but I knew eventually my health could begin anew.

Emotions are hazardous when you ride the waves

through turmoil. Negativism under stress while grieving, equals a perfect chance for another bad breakdown. Seizure drugs caused emotional outbreaks, which did not help either. Initially, drowning sounded pretty good most of the time. Other than hair loss, other physical complications affecting my body continually attacked me, and the pharmacy team was there to help me. Love flowed through everyone and made me feel special.

Chemo was humbling. Learning to not care what you looked like was nasty medicine to choke down. Doctors directed my days and I followed orders just to stay alive. Statistics were scary, so while in fear, I continued to float as sessions were almost over. I had dwell on how Christ suffered and was humiliated by enemies and friends, so I had to learn how to react as He did.

God chose to brighten my days and lighten the load during chemotherapy. Our daughter chose to get married in Hawaii. We had given them our timeshare week for a honeymoon in Honolulu and now all of us were going. It was good for me to get away and focus on joy. We were all in the ceremony, with our two year old grand-daughter as the flower girl. She and I had fun at the beach. I did not take off my wig, because I thought it might scare her. As I look back, she probably wouldn't have cared at all.

God organized an Aglow conference in Seattle to uplift my Spirit. Most of the women knew I was having treatments, and did not expect me to be there. Though my immune system was shaky, God knew a gathering of praise and worship with fellow sisters in Christ was the best medicine for me for my healing of shattered emotions.

The ending session of chemo was finally here. I could now ring the bell in the doctor's office as I'd watched others doing, wishing each time it was me. The sign at the bell read, "I have finished the treatment at the clinic. As I ring the bell, it signifies a body healed, a spirit renewed and a new hope for a brighter tomorrow." It was a very peaceful feeling.

Then I thought radiation would be a picnic next to chemo. I met new nurses and CNA's who were ready for the go-ahead. I would find again there was no privacy. I had nothing to hide anymore as the young men working in radiation began placing X's all over the breast area and on my back in different colored ink. The hospital was close to our house and walking was an option, but my body was too tired and worn down.

The staff hid themselves as radiation went right through my breast area and my back. It never hurt at all, but after 29 days, the burned skin peeled deeply for a long time making me raw on both sides. It was hard to sleep comfortably and I wore clothes that just hung on me. Mammograms happened every three months and there had to be concern always, for I knew a few friends who had experienced the recurrence of cancer coming back and haunting their sanity.

Strong faith can knock doubts out faster than anything. You never know what will happen in the game of life, but Jesus holding your hand is a special gift that not all experience because they don't know Him.

Chapter 24

Rising to a New Level

In 1974 after the seizures began again, I called for help wanting anyone to listen. Now I needed to be with people who would answer problems as they arose. Roger and my friend Sharon walked me through the recent chemo fires. Sharon had a heart of gold and a sweet listening ear. She would call and come over without my even asking her.

The devil thought he had won the battle, but I was standing firm trusting God was bigger than any problem that could come against me. God was still on the throne. I love Micah 7:8 which states, "Don't gloat over me my enemy, though I have fallen, I will rise. Though I sit in darkness, the Lord will be my light."

I needed a rubber raft to hold onto, while feeling the water of circumstances pull me down. God does protect you when you allow Him to guide with His light to carry you on into your destiny. I never had walked by myself in great turmoil before. During the other major valleys I had experienced, my parents, Roger or friends made decisions for my health. I was unaware of the dangers because my consciousness disappeared for a few moments.

However now, I felt God had promoted me to a new level. He was giving me the reins to direct myself to make decisions on my own. I asked and discussed ideas with others, but I had the right to say yes or no to anything. It was quite an honor to be given this responsibility. I knew He could lead me into victory through prayer. I had to swim upstream or go belly up and die. Being weak while treading water made it easy to sink; however, sinking was not an option anymore.

If I felt the need to talk, Jesus was there. My new life was emerging like a butterfly coming out of the cocoon. I sought Jesus more fervently as I was able to develop a greater sense of compassion for others. When Jesus calls us to the cross, you can't be like Him without the pain. I wanted to love in new depths and learn how to be a useful vessel to uplift others. I loved the verse from Nehemiah 8:10, "The joy of the Lord is my strength." The joy He brought me helped me walk on water.

I did feel joy knowing I had actually finished the race. The hot flames would now cease, and fear, tension and stress would be erased. Job 10:12 states, "You gave me life and showed me kindness." Second Timothy 4:7 says, "I have fought the good fight, I have finished the race, I have kept the faith." My reward had come. I had survived the nasty ordeal.

You come out of trials to enter a place of revelation, wisdom and fruitfulness. While in the furnace of affliction . . . prisons of testing, battlegrounds of temptations and trials, you are dying to this world and growing hungry to become more intimate with Christ to know His heart and His voice. You may not ever understand the mysteries and troubles, but if your heart is fully set on following Christ, you can rest assured God has purpose in all of it. He wants to bring you into His kingdom.

My new life was just beginning. My hair came back very slowly. It was spring and I'd had enough of wigs. What was I trying to hide? Everyone knew my hair was gone. The unveiling was about to happen. Any pride I had was now extinguished. We were at Roger's brother's house and I came downstairs without my wig and they looked stunned. I had finally pulled the plug and really did not care anymore what I looked like.

I was able to see I had been a broken vessel God used to prepare me for my destiny. I could glorify God in my body and bring cheer out of sadness. God knew I needed humbling and He did lift me up. We were blessed with a mighty victory. The cancer trial made me stronger, more compassionate and Christ-like. I was like a grape getting crushed to be used for another purpose for the body . . . like an alabaster jar that needed to be broken.

I needed to ask the Holy Spirit for forgiveness for

saying awful things about hating myself and wanting to die. There is a song we sing at church that has these words, "Take my life and let it be, all for you and for your glory." God could and would use me like I had always dreamed.

I had just needed more molding in the potter's hand, so I could do more for Him than ever before. I needed to preserve the anointing to be able to break through out into a new territory. The enemy has no clue where God is taking you. I had to persevere to finish the plan He had laid out for me . . . the Author and Finisher of my faith.

My Spirit was high, however, when I needed another mammogram five months later, it brought on fear quickly. The whole cancer experience had brought Roger and me closer with Jesus right in the middle, holding us both up. Letting go was quite a challenge, but I needed cleansing throughout by being.

Walking right in the fire, with Jesus holding your hand is more difficult than one could ever imagine. Jesus planned your entire life prior to conception. Human comprehension cannot understand why a loving God full of mercy would allow cancer cells to invade the human body. Many questions that bewilder us now will all have answers as our blinders will finally be removed in glory.

God sometimes needs to use strict discipline to help us grow closer to Him. Having the "cancer experience" helped me see His love flowing into me through outsiders and friends. I was simply not conscious of anyone helping while seizures occurred most of my adult life.

Prior to cancer, I had certain desires and needs, but now they were not important anymore. I developed a whole new outlook on life. I saw myself in a new light; the old was gone and the new me was shining bright. The devil meant only harm to break out, and God only brought good out of the evil that was intended.

Chapter 25

I Needed to Learn More

Do not try to be someone else or give up on life. If you think you have no value (which I did throughout the trials), you'll pray with less faith and conclude that the promises of God are for everyone else except you.

You should appreciate what God gives you and develop it. You should focus on your potential, not your limitations. You should have courage to be different and to be a God-pleaser, not a people pleaser.

Learn to handle criticism; let it develop and not hinder you. Each time you conquer fear, you can get self-respect and a new level of confidence. God cannot be pleased without faith, so make a commitment to develop faith.

When storms come, learn to see Jesus in them, and obey what He tells you. Refuse to be intimidated, and do what others in the boat would be afraid to do. Finally, believe in the impossible and give Christ your life to do whatever He wants to help you find your destiny.

Tough times bring on true character. The life of Christ is reproduced in us. Our shaky theology is changed into a set of convictions that help us handle things, rather than escape.

Perseverance produces a willingness to accept whatever comes and a determination to stand firm, and have insight to see God in it all. Without insight, we stumble and fall and God is grieved. With insight we survive and conquer and God is glorified. Our minds need to be renewed daily so we can see our problems as God sees them.

Our sorrow, failures and disappointments are very real, but they are also raw material for transformation. The Lord can and will accomplish this in His time. We will dance, for God will step in and bring our joy into dancing for Him and that brings Him the glory He deserves. We must wait, believe and remember His promises are for us forever.

My Mom watched and saw firsthand how I handled life during and after the diagnosis of breast cancer. She saw me very ill and later getting my life back together again. We went to visit her during my chemo, but my weakness caused the time to be shortened. She always said I looked good. I am grateful she had great care herself with a staff who loved her.

God's definition of "quickly" and ours are not the same. Delays work perseverance in us. Endurance is crucial for our character development that

God is willing to delay even important answers to prayers to help our transformation. So we shouldn't interpret divine delays as signs of divine reluctance. Delays are tools to perfect our faith. He looks for tenacity in our faith that prevails in spite of delays and setbacks. He seeks to create perseverance within us that outlasts a test of time that grows stronger during delays.

I never had to be concerned if I was not able to visit Mom because of my health issues. I believe she was blessed by seeing that her Janie could fight through the cancer battle, with the support of her caring husband. God's grace and mercy had allowed us again to blow the shofar, to chant and to shout about our newest victory. To God be the glory, great things He has done!

Part Six

CLAIMING VICTORY

Chapter 26

Bilateral Hip Revision?

The first hip surgery was done in 2006 and breast cancer had attacked in 2007. Now I chose to get the other hip done in 2008. There was no severe pain, but I was limping because of uneven legs and it was wearing down the weak bones.

Roger's job was at stake, and we knew surgery would be covered under our medical plan if we did it now. My doctor would try again to level my hips. The surgery went well. Walking was easy with no need for therapy. I felt the surgery was all behind me because the implants last 20 years. Roger dressed me and put on elastic stretch stockings to stop possible blood clots, prior to going to work.

I could not bend over three months because of hip dislocation. I got used to the walker and grabber again, but this would be the end of it. I was glad the human body has just two hips! After deep incisions healed, I could drive again. I went swimming for exercise while chatting with friends treading water and later swam laps. When the snow melted, I could be in the garden again without any pain involved.

While driving down to Florida to stay away from ice and cold, my surgeon called and told me I had "dangerously high blood levels of cobalt and chromium." I hadn't even heard of lab testing for those chemicals. What was he talking about? He said the dangers with metal on metal involved the parts rubbing together releasing toxins into my bloodstream anytime my body was in motion.

The surgery had been done well, but the metal parts he had used were faulty and were later recalled. My levels of chromium were 79, and cobalt was 29, and they are supposed to be zero. My clean blood was being poisoned! A major side effect of cobalt poisoning was possible seizure activity. Did this mean I should give up exercise just to stop toxins?

Friends suggested trying other therapies to avoid more surgery. There were drugs available without prescription to help rid toxins out of my system. They even suggested sauna baths, rub-on skin creams, or ion foot baths. Just sitting in salt water at beaches drew toxins out. Taking extra drugs to rid toxins could cause problems with my existing seizure drugs. I decided to forget the idea because it could cause seizures to recur. It had been over 15 years without any, so why start a nightmare on purpose?

I had no pain while walking and I thought it was totally ridiculous to even pursue the need for surgery. There had to be other ways to get the poisons out. I had no fear but I was never told toxins could eventually kill me.

My doctor said my MRI results showed fluid around the sockets, so they could dislocate. I overlooked his warnings, because this wasn't going to happen to me. Sound familiar? These toxins could do damage to my brain, heart, kidneys and liver. I continued to run from the truth and kept running. I saw no reason to go to the hospital when I felt fine. I shared concerns with family and friends. My brother Tom, who had been a hospital administrator 35 years and now retired, was concerned about me and thought I should have them removed.

It was now December 2010. We rented a place near Venice, Fla., where my parents had lived. We had plans to be in Maui in March and then see our daughter Liz and husband Ryan in Arizona on the way home. I did not want to fall on Wisconsin ice which could damage my hips.

Dramatic changes would take place in my body in 2011. It was March and I was overtired from an all-night flight from Maui. Then it happened. While we were sitting in Liz's kitchen in Tucson, I had a seizure. It was different than the kind I had for 16 years. I used to collapse while standing, but this was a facial grimace and stare. I still had no clue anything had happened.

Roger and Liz were in shock as I came out of it. We put it off as being overtired and wouldn't happen again. Wrong. We found a neurologist who increased Lamictal in small amounts, but I knew I was on more immediately. I felt dizzy and spaced out. It had to be taken after lunch, versus bedtime, which made it more noticeable.

I had an Aglow trip to Israel planned in early May, and this handicap would not stop me. I was not aware of seizure activity while there. There were about 80 of us, who were mostly leaders. God had me well protected. When I came back, our kids had arranged a large 40th anniversary party which we enjoyed immensely.

Later, Roger surprised me with an anniversary trip to Italy, staying at a 400 year-old farmhouse for a week on the Umbrian border, far away from city life, and then another week in Rome. Yes, I was tired and seizures did continue, as the doctor kept slowly increasing the drug. My body was adjusting to more drugs, so it was not quite as noticeable.

Meanwhile, my brother Tom was working on my behalf. He had a friend who used to work for him in California, Dr. Dave Dodgin, an orthopedic surgeon specializing in hip revisions, now working in Austin, Texas. Since surgery was now lingering over my whole being, Tom suggested seeing Dave for a second opinion. Roger and I chose to meet and discuss options with him. In August we flew to Austin to seek his advice. We learned he had done revisions before the sockets were recalled, because he said "they were bad from the beginning."

In Austin it was 110 degrees and humid, but

just hearing him suggest ideas to help me made the unbearable heat quite refreshing. He suggested the frontal anterior approach to surgery, versus my deep posterior incisions, with little or no danger of hip dislocation. It was a pencil-like slit with muscles stretched versus cutting through muscles over a four-hour surgery.

I was finally accepting the reality of this new drama that was about to unfold. I realized there was no other choice. I soon learned that an international lawsuit had developed causing the implants to be recalled due to widespread problems. Unfortunately, I had two of them.

When we met with Dr. Dodgin, I mentioned I was coming to Houston for an Aglow conference in October. So I suggested surgery right after the conference on October 5. After the conference, Roger would fly to Houston and drive me to Austin and get this taken care of, with Jesus as the Surgeon and Dr. Dodgin assisting Him.

He told us the bad metal sockets would be replaced with ceramic in plastic cups. He would just use glue and staples, versus layers of intricate stitching, which would make healing faster. Since he said he would do both at once, he could use a computer to level my legs, which had never worked before. This way it would involve only one surgical procedure versus two.

We also learned that my brother and his wife Ruth wanted to join us in Austin prior to surgery. Spending time at the conference would also be uplifting, with dancing during worship and having friends pray with me. I felt encouraging peace in my soul. I jokingly said, "I would be so high, the doctors would have to tie me down to the table." Ironically, that is exactly what they do for intricate surgery, so I would never move an inch.

God always has a perfect plan. The devil does enjoy hurting people and has no trouble provoking fear into any Christian who seems to be managing life well. My faith life became stronger in every deep valley. You grow more fervently while trouble brews.

Prior to this new testing, my emotions took the best of me and fear fell all over me. Now after having experienced crisis many years now and having seen God by my side, I felt I was ready to walk on water. Whatever comes our way, we will rise above it all. Where I belong Lord is at Your feet praising You.

While in Israel, I claimed healing in Cana where Jesus turned water into wine. We went to the Pool of Bethesda, where another Biblical healing occurred. John 5:5–6, "One who was there had been an invalid for 38 years. When Jesus saw him lying there... he asked him, "Do you want to get well?" It was quite exciting to be there where a miracle happened. People laid hands on me there and I knew in my heart there would be no need for hip surgery.

We arrived home realizing hip surgery was imminent. Quite disappointing. My faith had skyrocketed and boom. So what did that mean? Surgery was going to happen because God was in control. I had to step up to the plate, accept His plan and hold on, knowing He had never failed me before. Psalm 138: 7–8 states, "Though I walk in the midst of trouble, you preserve my life…, with your right hand you save me. The Lord will perform his purpose for me." I had to strongly believe that He would perfect that which concerns me.

Chapter 27

Time for More Testing

I never thought about hip surgery as being "in a battle" before. The devil wanted me in a bad position, hoping I would come out paralyzed, with no victory in sight. I was trusting I would walk out a winner with no complications. I Samuel 17:47 states, "For the battle is the Lord's, and He will give all of you into our hands." God was in control.

God does not always calm the waters. He does not keep the floods from coming or put out fires. But He does promise that He will walk with you through it all. The trial will not destroy or consume you. Walk on, and you will come out on the other side with Him beside you.

I had peace knowing this trial would go well. Too many pieces of the puzzle had been placed together before surgery, so I knew God's Hand was on me. With the posterior incisions I had before, I'd have to go through two separate surgeries, six months apart and not been able to bend or sit comfortably for three months each time. Going to Texas, using the new anterior approach, both hips would be done in the same surgery, which would also help the doctor level my uneven legs.

There would be challenges ahead. I wrote an email to a good friend staying, "I wish it was all over." She responded with an answer I did not understand, so I called her. She said, "God has reasons for life's stages, and there would be something coming later on, so I could see it was good for me. I should get ready for an upgrade." An "upgrade?" Just what I needed to hear, and quite exciting! He is a great big God and knows everything that is going on. I knew in my heart that I could make it again.

God found us a law firm who would take care of all financial expenses incurred before, during and after surgery. It was estimated that more than 7,200 cases were involved internationally. I'm sure we all trusted they would be good for 20 years.

Many years of tears have made me bolder and stronger than ever before. I am ready to tell the world about God's great love for them. Never will the Lord tell anyone, get hold of yourself, stand up and take your medicine, grit your teeth and dry your tears. He stores every tear in His eternal container.

Battles are not meant to just cause tribulation, but to bring victory. They are pathways to possess God's promises. I knew I couldn't give the enemy an open door so he could have his way. Sinking was not an option. The world will see His glory shown in my life and know that God has great power.

I would stand on and totally give my all to God. He had brought me this far and I knew nothing bad would happen. Any possible problems that could arise, would all go smoothly and at the exact time. The joy of the Lord would be my strength. Any evil spirits of unbelief and fear were gone. Victory was in the making.

Having peace about this surgery gave me victory. I had to keep my eyes focused on how Christ would react. He chose God's will in suffering for all of us. I could handle this. I was told while going through struggles, you grow in character.

Before my battle began, I knew the devil was not afraid of me, but Christ who lived in me. I knew worshipping and praying were necessary for battle. All victory comes from seeking God, and when you find Him, you can let His presence fill your spirit with peace.

There was freedom knowing His will would be done and nothing could stop it. Although there were some "fleshly thoughts" of fear, they disappeared quickly. I just felt blessed that it would soon be over.

Chapter 28

Possible Victory Again?

The Aglow conference in Houston was planned (the timing and location) it seemed just for me. The speakers spoke what I needed to hear and all that was said and done brought peace to my soul. There was praise and worship while I danced freely and forgot anything the devil was trying to throw my way. I knew God wanted me to survive and be fruitful. I expected victory. I found friends everywhere who knew my surgery was in a few days. I wanted to see their smiles or get a hug.

After the conference was over, Roger and I drove to Austin. When my brother and his wife arrived from California, reality hit hard. I was sad they had to share this hardship, because we don't have much time with them. I didn't want to burden them with the affairs of surgery.

After checking in the hotel, I was in our room alone. My emotions let go and bottled up tears hit hard because reality of surgery was knocking on my door. I was overtired and poisons spread into all my major organs, causing them to work overtime. Seizure activity continued, but because of the increased drug amounts, my brain was calmed from over-activity. Deep inside my Spirit, I knew it would be all over shortly.

Surgery was the next day. We arrived at the hospital at 5 a.m. and I saw my name on the board with the time of surgery. We knew for months that the hip sockets were faulty and now the game playing was over. It was truly amazing that my body was able to hold on with large amounts of poison in it until October 2011. Swimming upstream would no longer be necessary, for total healing was now at hand. I felt the prayers going through my entire being.

The surgery went well and pain was not an issue, because of an epidural. A few days later there was noticeably more pain while walking and moving from the bed to the bathroom. While motionless, pain was not evident. I decided to stop the chronic painkillers for they had worse side-effects than pain itself. After four hours in surgery, the stretched muscles felt like daggers going into me, every time I got in and out of bed. It hurt just to touch the thigh area with my fingers. But lying still most of the time, I seemed to be pain-free.

Within a few days, I became very weak, shaky and unable to stand. The doctor was aware of the loss of two units of contaminated blood. New blood was ordered immediately and the transfusion took over five hours to replenish it. Now the new clean blood in me could mix together and water down the poisoned bad blood. This would make it wash out of my system more quickly.

I stayed in the hospital four days with tests to see if blood clots had formed, but there were none. I was moved to rehabilitation, which was connected to the hospital. The facility had a heated therapy pool for exercise. How perfect. I had no swim suit, but they provided cut-off shirts and loose shorts to wear. I could float around with a noodle and water walk in 90-degree water.

The pool had tread mills and weight lifts you use in the water. They had put clear wide mailing tape over my two nine-inch incisions that had been glued and stapled shut. Your body is buoyant and you feel no pain while exercising. This therapy lasted for six one-hour days in water, along with two hours daily on land. Yes, I did feel the pain and my stretched muscles were not happy. The human body can adjust to pain and is able to withstand heavy burdens placed on it.

I walked and practiced getting into and out of a car and walking on different surfaces with the walker. After the staples were taken out in 10 days and the Coumadin levels were right, we could now head home. We drove our rented car back to Houston and then flew home, which became a nightmare when it came to pain. There was no room in the front seats promised to us. My muscles were very tight and were bent into bad positions. My knees hit the wall and I could not move or stretch my legs out straight, which could have helped immensely. Praise God, we made it home and I slept well in our own bed with our kitty.

About a month after surgery, the pulled muscles let go more, but it took longer than I expected for the pain to cease. Because my one longer leg prior to surgery had been dominant, extra pain happened just getting used to being the same length now. After six weeks, X-rays of both hips were done and sent to Texas. The results were perfect for we knew Jesus was guiding the doctor's hands.

I know He had me very well prepared for this last surgery. Many times before I fought through trials. In this last trial I saw myself in a new way. I did not fight it and went through it all in peace.

We were blessed to be in Florida again following surgery for a few months. There seemed to be no stress down in Florida and relaxing was what we both needed from all those months prior to and after the surgery. We lost many hours of sleep and God was gifting us now, refreshing us and creating wonderful happiness.

Trials were the fruit of the seasons where God taught me to fight. I had learned to get fed up with the devil's nonsense and to take heed over his works quickly. Trials bring on promotion. You will be a victor if you do not quit. God allows you to face what you are prepared to face with Him. The measuring line usually is higher than we thought. But, in a season of trials, God offers you promotion: to step into a new level of boldness and dominion with Christ. He is giving you what you asked for, while you're being unaware of what the journey was going to be. You must trust that God will capitalize on every trial and triumph to shape and transform you into Christ's image.

Chapter 29

Mom's Secrets Are Known

Through my mother's 91 years, blessings and hardships occurred, but she had great faith walking through anything. Quite a woman to behold and the type you'd desire to follow in her footsteps. We enjoyed her last years living near our Wisconsin home. Everyone she met enjoyed quality time with her as we did. Her honesty and love flowed out of her and she was loved by all.

The days of her life were now closing, as she consumed less food for a variety of reasons. We ate meals with her and she saw her ground food next to our whole food and pushed her plate away. She had been a great cook, and food played a major role in her life. Losing her joy of eating was a downfall and why I think she decided to lose her will to live.

The staff tried everything they could think of that she loved to eat, but water, milk and M&M's became her main diet. Her Spirit was alive but her drive to keep going fell apart. Her clothes just hung on her. She had one last request: oyster stew, like she had as a young girl. Finding oysters in central Wisconsin wasn't easy but we made it for her and she consumed it immediately. How she even digested it, without having any real food for months, is beyond me.

My brother came more often, knowing she had given up her will to live. The day before she died, Tom chose to ask her two questions. He knew her more intimately and had spent many hours alone with both my parents. He asked, "What was your best memory?" Having children was her answer.

What was her worst? I guessed having Dad ill most of their married life. When he had the tongue bi-section, they should have moved directly to an assisted living because the stress on Mom was horrible for many years. Dad wanted no outside care and wanted to stay at home. So that is what happened. The last month of his life he moved into a nursing home and soon went home to be with Jesus.

My guess was wrong. My near-death experience traumatized her whole emotional being for many years. Initially I felt remorse and my heart was heavy, because of the burden I had created for all involved. After dwelling on her answer months later, I now saw things differently.

God had opened doors of victory like never before. They grew closer to each other and Jesus. They learned to trust Jesus and stronger faith developed that was theirs forever. Their friends held them up and onto them when they were almost broken, which made them stronger. They did not institutionalize me, but watched me slowly heal at home. They saw me come back to life though doctors warned them it would never happen. My damaged brain was healed and they experienced joy when I received my college diploma. My wonderful marriage with Roger and two special children were gifts to me. With God, nothing was impossible.

Their having walked through my illness prepared the way when my Dad was diagnosed with cancer a year later. He suffered for years, but having seen God work in my life gave them hope for his healing. Their faith was strong as they faced calamities, walking graciously through every fiery ordeal they faced. God was their strength when trouble brewed.

Watching them walk through fire, gave me courage that I could make it as seizures seemed never ending. I had the joy of seeing how an unapproved FDA drug at the time would work for me. Jesus was my healer, and praise and worship became part of me. Though I never knew my parents intimately, their faith kept me strong. We will have time in heaven and we will grow in intimacy and love, learning more about each other then. I'll have the joy and ability then to tell them how really special they are for all of eternity.

Chapter 30

Trying to Remain Strong

I lost my Dad and now my Mom. But I was told I shouldn't let circumstances dictate me. Saints can endure hardships without altering their identity. You may seem to be in chains, but remain God's righteous worker just for Him. Can you imagine Paul giving up saying, "I am done, it is over?" No way, he just gets bolder, not intimidated or ashamed. Paul was not chained in his Spirit, he was only bound in the flesh.

In Philippians 4:13 he states, "I can do all things through Him who gives me strength." I did find I became stronger through each trial and much bolder to share what God was doing. I had to remember to come boldly to His throne and ask for all the grace and mercy He could give me to walk the storm out.

The Spirit had to help me understand this truth, because the coming days ahead would be the greatest ones I ever had. I had to know I would make mistakes, but not to be shaken, because I had the victory and was to live in it.

I guess I was just plain tired of being the sick one, always in hospitals, doctor offices and physical therapy. With my first surgeries, I was walking without pain. I forgot I had new fake hips. There were no set-backs or problems with either surgery. I had even fallen and landed right on the hip area without damage. I was scared while waiting to hear what the X-rays read. God had protected me.

Why did I receive two "recalled" sockets that both had to come out? God made the human spirit to be enduring. Trials have made me who I am today. Painful experiences cause growth on a high-level and make you able to grow more in virtue and strength. They press and squeeze us until we are crushed until you are right in the face of Jesus. Give up control and then He takes over. Faith grows as we push through trials. This war with the enemy was not over, but I had already won. I was created a winner and I had great endurance. I had to succeed.

God had kept me alive through many catastrophes, accidents, illnesses and helped me keep on fighting. Psalm 34:15 states, "The eyes of the Lord are on the righteous and His ears are attentive to their cry. Verse 17 continues, "The righteous cry out, and the Lord hears them; he delivers them from all their troubles." I had to stand firm and know He had me in the palm of His Hands. II Chronicles 16:9 states, "For the eyes of the Lord range throughout the earth to strengthen those whose hearts are fully committed to Him." I had to read His Word to be encouraged daily.

Why is it that humans long for a life without difficulties? Oak trees grow strong in contrary winds and diamonds are made under pressure. We only see calamity as bad. God's purposes in our lives take time to form as I have always seen. In Psalm 70, David cries out for immediate extraction from his difficult troubles . . . like I wanted to do so many times. I wanted Him to do something right now. You have no interest in being an oak tree or diamond, but just surviving for the present.

I guess I do not remember crying out for help, but being so drugged for so long, a lot slips from my memory. I did cry inwardly and sought Him in prayer. I read His word and enjoyed being in Bible studies with wonderful friends. They really cared and spent much time listening to my needs. Even if success seemed to be impossible, I had to seek for God's intervention. I did desire to go on living. Calling out to God meant I wanted His help because my life was worthwhile.

God often seems slow. Was it because victories gained after a hard fought battle are more enjoyed? Or would I learn the lesson better? God could be interweaving plans for other people's lives with yours, like for me, meeting Lori, because I had fought the trial that she was starting and needed help I could now give her.

I had to avoid false thinking because of His slow answers. It was not because He was powerless or He did not care. He was not sleeping, indifferent or unconcerned. He had my best interest in mind. God was too wise to be mistaken, and too loving to be unkind. While waiting, focus can shift back and forth from God to yourself, and back to your problem. Wondering why and what to do is always there. God gives you freedom to keep asking for Him to hurry up. Delays don't come from His disinterest, but from His knowledge, that even as trials make oaks and diamonds, so also they produce saints.

I always prayed for help when disaster struck. I knew I had no resources to get myself out of any problem. I knew if He did not help me, I was done for. So I asked for deliverance in whatever it was and that I would be grateful for His help.

I was on the sidelines, waiting for action. God could give me needed rest to build me up, but to also discipline me. He could be drawing me close to himself by removing danger from me. He also could be preparing me to help others in similar situations.

I was to be delighted in God and know He would satisfy my heart. I was to commit everything to Him, trust Him, because He was my help. It caused me to be able to see Him in a new light and see justice someday. Psalm 46:10 states, "Be still and know that I am God." God would act.

Waiting would be the hard part. I was not to worry. That would be easier said than done. I wanted to be useful to Him in bringing in the harvest, so that all would come to know Him as I continued in the upcoming struggle. I would need more of

God to complete this task. I was being transformed inside, by the working of God's hand, while He renewed my mind. My heart was being changed and I would find newness, a radiance of God in me. I could not allow worry to overtake me, but I had to trust wholly in Him.

I also read about how God delights in me. He delivered me from my enemies and sorrows because I was precious to Him. Psalm 18:19 states, "He rescued me because He delighted in me." Psalm 147:11 states, "the Lord delights in them those who fear Him, who put their hope in His unfailing love." Actually, almost every Psalm has great comfort and can make your faith stronger.

I had to believe there was deliverance from every battle that rages in your soul, which was the secret to entering into rest God promised you. It must be held onto, as a truth in your heart, so that you can withstand your trials of life. God will take care of you when you give Him your life.

Conclusion

Joy Comes After Mourning

I'd like to share some thoughts with you after reading my testimony. I am hopeful it has given encouragement for you to fight on and know there will be a better tomorrow.

Joy is hard to explain. It is not necessarily just a positive attitude or pleasant emotion. Joy is linked with delight. It is an emotion and a fruit. There are levels of joy including gladness, contentment and cheerfulness. This joy rises above circumstances and focuses on God's character, which can release His emotion through us when we experience His will. When you know Jesus as His child, joy is produced by His Spirit. This joy can help us see our future. This is what makes joy different than happiness. It can cause us to rise above sorrow and loss.

Many people have asked how I was able to remain at peace and keep a smile on my face through seemingly stressful situations. Though I had to bite the bullet through chemo, those who were very close knew total peace was not there, but God gave me grace to walk through it all in faith. Trusting and believing were difficult at times and some valleys were severely deep. Sometimes my hope dwindled seeing nothing but another battle being waged. However, hearing sermons or meeting someone who had walked through the healing I needed, was proof to me they had succeeded, which gave me the incentive to go for the prize and also be a victor.

If the devil can remove your joy, he can remove your strength. Strength means the ability to stand firm when attacks come. Keeping and holding onto strength is key to the Spirit-filled life. Nehemiah 8:10 says, "The joy of The Lord is your strength."

How do you handle warfare with the devil? The faster you submit to God and His will, you can resist the devil more easily. I fought the devil by myself way too long, because I did not know Jesus and how powerful He could be for me. If I had just learned to stop trying to make things go my way and let God work, I believe healing could have happened a lot faster. Wisdom from God was just not there.

While seeing no answers while trouble was brewing is when God should take the reins. Letting go is necessary so His grace can shelter us from the devil's attacks. Submission protects you from many roadblocks the devil can set up for you.

Our trials we walk through can become a blessing in God's hand and can produce fulfillment in our lives. Going through chemo and seizures can become a joy-filled moment when you see reasons behind it and what God was doing through it and then thank Him for it. Knowing chemo stopped cancer and drugs ended seizures, I realized it was worth the agony of having gone through it. I do enjoy freedom like never before. They were all set-backs, but God got the victory, as I did. The harsh memories of pain have all subsided and my joy has come. It was the gift of grace that can now be seen in me for a lifetime.

There is a level of joy we would never experience if we never suffered loss. The deeper the sorrow, the more capacity for joy we seem to have. When loss happens, nothing seems to be the same. The Bible is full of references about mourning turned to joy. Here are a few I held onto. Psalm 30:5 tells us, "Weeping may remain for a night, but rejoicing comes in the morning." Verse 11 continues, "You turned my wailing into dancing; you removed my sackcloth and clothed me with joy." I do love danc-ing and it did set me free many times, giving me total peace.

Sorrow and joy are always linked together. Maybe because the deeper the sorrow, the more we experi-ence joy. We may only see tears and sorrow of the night, but He has planned a beautiful morning full of joy.

Joy works like medicine and brings healing to us in many ways. By just looking at things positively, we see the situation as good. Waiting to see what

God has in mind is always good wisdom. Do not get your eyes off the Lord and His will for your life, or your whole spirit can fall apart. That is exactly what the devil wants. Do not let him have his desires.

My prayer is that all who have read my story can become joy carriers that God created us to be. Enter into the joy realm and break forth and share Jesus with everyone you meet. He is the greatest joy of my life, and I am trusting you have seen the purpose for sharing my testimony with whomever wants to see God at work and His unfathomable love for all humanity.

End

CPSIA information can be obtained at www.ICGtesting.com
Printed in the USA
LVOW05s2310010114

367591LV00009B/212/P